# Managing a Genealogical Project

# Managing a Genealogical Project

**William Dollarhide**

A Complete Manual for the Management and Organization
of Genealogical Materials

Genealogical Publishing Co., Inc.
Baltimore

Originally published 1988
Revised and updated 1991
Updated 1999
Copyright © 1988, 1991, 1999
William Dollarhide
All rights reserved. No part of this publication
may be reproduced, in any form or by any means,
including electronic reproduction or reproduction
via the Internet, except by permission of the publisher.
Published by Genealogical Publishing Co., Inc.
1001 N. Calvert St., Baltimore, MD 21202
Second printing, 2001
Library of Congress Catalogue Card Number 88-80781
International Standard Book Number 0-8063-1222-X
*Made in the United States of America*

## Dedication

To Joyce Hensen and Gary Toms

# Contents

## Section 1—Types of Genealogical Projects

## Section 2—Collecting References

**Contents** (continued)

## Section 3—Retrieving Notes and Compiling Family Sheets

## Section 4—Ahnentafel Numbering

## Section 5—Descendancy Numbering

## Section 6—Using a Computer

## Section 7—Presentation Techniques

## Appendix—Research Journals and Logs

## Master Forms (in back of book)

   1. Relationship Chart
   2. Reference Family Data Sheet (RFDS)
   3. Compiled Family Data Sheet (CFDS)
   4. CFDS Continuation Sheet
   5. Master Data Sheet (MDS)
   6. Research Log
   7. Ancestor Table
   8. Pedigree Ancestor Index
   9. Research Journal
  10. Correspondence Log

# Preface

*Managing a Genealogical Project* is an outgrowth of The Dollarhide System for Genealogical Records, a manual system used by thousands of genealogists all across the country. The specific methods of organizing genealogical materials have evolved over a period of years and have proved to be very beneficial to anyone compiling family research of any kind.

This is not a *how-to* book on starting a family tree, but beginning genealogists may appreciate the techniques described and begin organizing their records systematically to avoid serious problems later. Most experienced genealogists are faced with "piles" of paper—the beginner will soon find out what that means—and if some method is not found early in the collection stage, the paperwork may become overwhelming.

To make the suggestions and ideas come together, a set of master forms, designed to be photocopied and used, has been included in this book These forms will be described in each section of the book and will give the genealogist a practical answer to organizing genealogical material systematically.

The book is divided into seven sections. Each section gives specific suggestions for organizing an important aspect of a genealogical project, from the first notes written to the published book or presentation of the findings in a genealogical report. The sections to follow are described briefly below:

## 1. Types of Genealogical Projects

Before learning how to manage any project, it is important to understand the nature of the project and its limits. This section describes different genealogical organizational problems and lists common terms used in the field of genealogy.

## 2. Collecting References

This section will describe techniques of collecting notes and documents in a logical scheme, using standard sheet sizes and creating pages in loose-leaf binders for easy retrieval.

## 3. Retrieving Notes and Compiling Family Sheets

This section will demonstrate methods of indexing names, places, events, etc., so that information can be retrieved quickly from the raw notes and documents. With all of the facts gathered, a family sheet can be prepared.

### 4. Ahnentafel Numbering

For a pedigree, the use of ahnentafel numbers will give every ancestor a discrete ID number. The ancestor/ahnentafel number can also be used to organize families. Ahnentafel numbers allow genealogists to quickly display information in a lineage, a surname line, a partial pedigree, or several other interesting arrangements—which makes the project easier to understand and control.

### 5. Descendancy Numbering

For preparing a descendancy, there are three standard numbering systems available to genealogists. These are described in detail. Also included is a method that shows how to integrate pedigree ancestors with their siblings and descendants in a combined numbering scheme.

### 6. Using a Computer

Even with the power of the personal computer, the task of computerizing a genealogical project will become a huge headache if the hard-copy files are not well managed first. This section describes some techniques to avoid the aspirin and allow the use of off-the-shelf database and word processor programs. Descriptions of the leading genealogical software, comparing their different features, have been included.

### 7. Presentation Techniques

Methods of presenting the project—graphically or using charts and narratives—have been included to show various ideas in presenting either a pedigree or descendancy.

❀   ❀   ❀

# Managing a Genealogical Project

# Section 1
# Types of Genealogical Projects

## Introduction

There are some important differences to identify when discussing genealogical projects. For example, a pedigree is completely different from a descendancy. There are projects that are limited to one lineage from either the pedigree or descendancy, or one-name studies which concentrate on people with the same surname. This section will describe these differences.

## A Pedigree

Most genealogists start with a pedigree, an identification of all direct ancestors for a person, that is, the parents, grandparents, great-grandparents, etc. It does not include uncles, aunts, nieces, nephews, or cousins of a person. A pedigree can be diagramed as shown in Figure 1 to identify the ancestors. (All names are fictitious.)

Note that James SMITH starts the pedigree. This could be called "the pedigree of James SMITH." Note also that only the direct ancestors of James SMITH are shown. Even though William SMITH and Elizabeth BROWN may

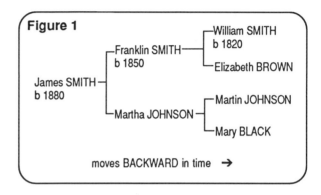

have had several children, only the pedigree child, Franklin SMITH, is shown on the diagram.

The position of ancestors on the diagram should follow some basic rules; for example, the male should always be in the upper position and the female in the lower position:

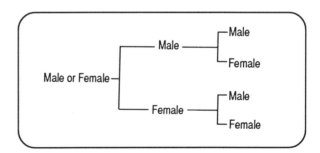

An important distinction about the pedigree is that it moves *backward* in time; that is, the first person is usually

1

someone alive today, and the ancestors of that person are identified moving from left to right, back in time, generation by generation.

# A Lineage

One line, or lineage, can be traced from the pedigree to highlight one particular line of ascent or descent, then reviewed as a separate project:

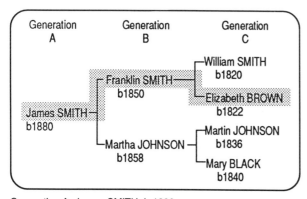

Generation A: James SMITH, b 1880
Generation B: Franklin SMITH, b1850
Generation C: Elizabeth BROWN, b1822

This lineage is just one of several that could be pulled from the pedigree. An advantage in identifying a lineage is that a relationship to a certain person back in time could be compiled without the need to showing the entire pedigree.

A lineage of one *surname* can also be traced from the pedigree so that a male line can be identified:

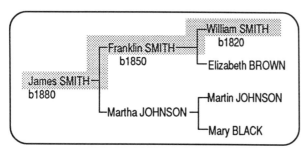

Smith Lineage:
    James SMITH, b1880
    Franklin SMITH, b1850
    William SMITH, b1820

# A Descendancy

A descendancy, sometimes called a "genealogy," is a completely different project from a pedigree. Those genealogists who have identified their pedigree lineage to a certain ancestor back in time may be intrigued with the many descendants besides themselves, and begin to prepare a comprehensive descent list, generation by generation, starting with that one person back in time. A diagram of a descendancy might appear as shown below:

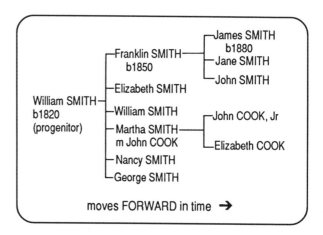

In the above example only a few persons have been extended with their descendants. However, the numbers of people who may be part of the descendancy can be staggering, and one must realize the scope of such a project compared with a simple pedigree.

For example, the pedigree moves back in time, and each step, or generation, reveals double the number of the previous step. Each ancestor was produced by a pair of ancestors, and the mathematics is quite orderly and simple to follow.

On the other hand, a descendancy has no known number of persons in each generation, and in large families, the numbers can build rapidly. It is not unusual to see several hundred descendants of a single person in just four or five generations. Each succeeding generation will continue to add hundreds, perhaps thousands, of descendants.

The important distinction about a descendancy is that it moves *forward* in time, starting with a person identified back in time somewhere. Unlike a pedigree, which moves backward in time, the descendancy must begin with a progenitor, followed by all descendants of that progenitor.

A lineage can be traced from the descendancy as well:

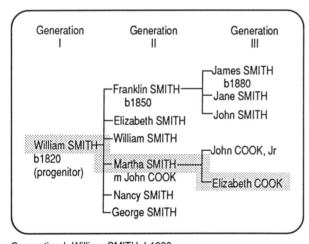

Generation I: William SMITH, b1820
Generation II: Martha (Smith) COOK
Generation III: Elizabeth COOK

A lineage may be traced from either the pedigree or the descendancy—in fact, an identical lineage is possible. But time is moving in opposite directions in each.

# Determining Relationships

Relationships can be determined from a descendancy in which two separate lineages are traced until a "common ancestor" has been found. In order for two people to be related, an ancestor must be shared by both persons. The lineage can be traced using either males or females, and must be a child, parent, grandparent, and so on.

*NOTE:*

*In the case of a pedigree, every person on the diagram is an ancestor of the first person. The other people share no direct relationship at all—unless two cousins marry and produce offspring, which means that at least one ancestor will appear more than once in the same pedigree.*

Relationships can be quickly identified using a special relationship chart if a common ancestor is known. A sample chart is shown on page 4. Two lineages are displayed on the sample chart. One is moving up, starting with the common ancestor (1), followed by A2, A3, A4, etc., and the other lineage is moving down, starting again with the common ancestor, then B2, B3, B4, etc. The box indicates the relationship between any two people from the two lineages.

For example, A6 and B6 would be 4th cousins. Or, the relationship of A6 to B7 would be 4th cousins, once removed. Persons the same number of steps (generations) removed from the common ancestor would either be siblings or full

# Relationship Chart

A relationship between two people can be determined if a common ancestor is known. The two lineages should both begin with the common ancestor, shown on the chart as number 1. Next, list two lineages, one line shown below as A2, A3, A4, etc., which moves up, and the other as B2, B3, B4, etc., which moves down. By tracing any two persons to a point in the box where the grey or white bands intersect, a legal relationship can be found. For example, A3 and B3 are first cousins, but A3 and B4 are first cousins, once removed.

LEGEND:

    N = niece or nephew to uncle or aunt.

    GN = Great niece or nephew.

2C 1R = second cousins, once removed.

3C 4R = third cousins, four times removed.

A10 — 7gr grandson/dau
A9 — 6gr grandson/dau
A8 — 5gr grandson/dau
A7 — 4gr grandson/dau
A6 — gr-gr-gr grandson/dau
A5 — gr-gr grandson/dau — JOHN A. DOLLARHIDE
A4 — great grandson/dau — OLEY E. DOLLARHIDE
A3 — grandson/dau — JOHN W. DOLLARHIDE
A2 — son/dau — JESSE DOLLARHIDE, Jr.

↑ LINEAGE A

1 COMMON ANCESTOR — JESSE DOLLARHIDE, Sr.

↓ LINEAGE B

| | A10 | A9 | A8 | A7 | A6 | A5 | A4 | A3 | A2 | |
|---|---|---|---|---|---|---|---|---|---|---|
| | 7GN | 6GN | 5GN | 4GN | 3GN | 2GN | GN | N | Siblings | B2 — son/dau — REV. JOHN DOLLARHIDE |
| | 1C 7R | 1C 6R | 1C 5R | 1C 4R | 1C 3R | 1C 2R | 1C 1R | 1st Cousins | N | B3 — grandson/dau — JOHN C. DOLLARHIDE |
| | 2C 6R | 2C 5R | 2C 4R | 2C 3R | 2C 2R | 2C 1R | 2nd Cousins | 1C 1R | GN | B4 — great grandson/dau — ALBERT R. DOLLARHIDE |
| | 3C 5R | 3C 4R | 3C 3R | 3C 2R | 3C 1R | 3rd Cousins | 2C 1R | 1C 2R | 2GN | B5 — gr-gr grandson/dau — WILLIAM DOLLARHIDE |
| | 4C 4R | 4C 3R | 4C 2R | 4C 1R | 4th Cousins | 3C 1R | 2C 2R | 1C 3R | 3GN | B6 — gr-gr-gr grandson — MEREDYTH DOLLARHIDE |
| | 5C 3R | 5C 2R | 5C 1R | 5th Cousins | 4C 1R | 3C 2R | 2C 3R | 1C 4R | 4GN | B7 — 4gr grandson/dau |
| | 6C 2R | 6C 1R | 6th Cousins | 5C 1R | 4C 2R | 3C 3R | 2C 4R | 1C 5R | 5GN | B8 — 5gr grandson/dau |
| | 7C 1R | 7th Cousins | 6C 1R | 5C 2R | 4C 3R | 3C 4R | 2C 5R | 1C 6R | 6GN | B9 — 6gr grandson/dau |
| | 8th Cousins | 7C 1R | 6C 2R | 5C 3R | 4C 4R | 3C 5R | 2C 6R | 1C 7R | 7GN | B10 — 7gr grandson/dau |

cousins, that is, 1st cousins, 2nd cousins, 3rd cousins, and so on. If the two people being compared are not the same number of steps away from the common ancestor, this is indicated as cousins, "once removed," "twice removed," "three times removed," and so on.

## Summary

There is a distinct difference between a pedigree and a descendancy. The pedigree moves back in time, identifying only the direct ancestors of one person. The descendancy moves forward in time, identifying all descendants of one progenitor. While the pedigree has a precise number of ancestors, doubling for each generation back in time, the descendancy has no known number of people for each generation.

In addition, a lineage from the pedigree or the descendancy may be of importance to a researcher. Understanding these differences will allow for organizing the records in a manner that will facilitate the handling of any project from a single source of documents and notes. In the next section, a method of collecting references will be shown, regardless of the type of genealogical project.

❖　❖　❖　❖　❖

# Glossary of Genealogical Relationships

Pedigree .......................... identification of ancestors

Pedigree ancestor .......... parent, grandparent, etc.

Direct ancestor .............. same as above

Ancestor .......................... same as above

Pedigree child ................ the sibling who continues the lineage of the pedigree

Collateral ........................ belonging to the same ancestral stock but not in a direct line of descent

Collateral siblings ......... brothers or sisters of the pedigree child

Collateral lines .............. descendants of collateral siblings (sometimes called "allied lines," "ancillary lines," or "parallel lines")

Common ancestor .......... belonging to or shared by two or more persons

Progenitor ...................... a person with descendants, or a person who begins a descendancy

Generation ...................... a body of persons comprising a single step in the descent from a single progenitor or more than one progenitor

Lineage .......................... one line of descent from a common ancestor

# Section 2
## Collecting References

### Piles of Paper

When genealogists first become interested in their family history, their collection of notes and documents is small and easy to handle. It will probably never get larger than a packet of papers unless they proceed further with the next steps in research. Taking these next steps is when the researcher discovers the wealth of information that is available, and the notes and documents begin to build rapidly.

After just a year or so, a diligent genealogist may have collected hundreds of pages of notes, representing many hours of library research, correspondence, or extracted information. If his stack of paper continues to grow without some control, as is typical with many genealogists, he will have to bring the research to a standstill and devise a method of controlling the paper. The cause of this typical problem is due to the nature of the project.

For example, one of the problems that hinders a genealogical project is the strange urge many researchers have acquired: they *must* create *families*. Nearly every genealogy teacher will stress the importance of the "Family Group Sheet" as the basic method of organizing records.

Yet the information that goes on a family sheet was first compiled from notes and documents. If a reference in a tax list to a person living alone in 1779 in North Carolina is all that is known about that person, it is impossible to learn anything more by filling out a family sheet, particularly if there is no information on the sheet except perhaps one person's name and approximate date of birth. The importance of the notes and documentation as the primary source of information cannot be overstated. Therefore, a means of collecting the source material into a retrievable form is essential. This all happens before family sheets can be prepared.

This leads to another problem universal to genealogists, again partly because of the nature of the project itself. Genealogists collect information for people who are relations as well as for non-relatives or those who are *suspected* to be relatives. This creates organizational questions: Should non-relatives be filed separately? Or, should ancestors be treated differently than collaterals? If research is conducted in such a way as to have the notes and documents well organized first, the problem of "who is who" need not be a hindrance.

## Solving the Paper-collecting Problem

The answer to many of these problems is to devise a collection system for notes and documents *only*, completely separate from anything else in the project. The solution lies in creating a simple filing system for every note, every census record, every deed, every will, every sheet of paper received in correspondence, and every other source collected in the research, regardless of what family the records may eventually reveal. In addition, family information can be compiled from the note collection system for a pedigree, a lineage, or a descendancy, giving the genealogist more flexibility should the project take a different direction.

There must, however, be some good, solid rules to follow in developing this filing system. This first filing system is for the *notes and documents*—not family sheets. Family sheets are indeed important and should be prepared when information about a particular family has been revealed. However, these sheets are not the source of the paper-collecting problem—the lack of a filing system independent of families may be the source of the problem.

## Identifying the Notes and Documents

Genealogical notes and documents are those extracts, photocopies, abstracts, and other handwritten notations acquired in research. The research collection system also includes documents received through the mail and correspon-

dence in which genealogical information has been revealed. This collection is for making sense of what is known about the family lines, and every single piece of information that has ever been collected should be included.

However, the originals of fragile archival materials, such as old photos, precious family documents, certificates, etc., should not be part of the note files. These originals should be stored in some other safe place, but the notes/documents collection should include copies of the originals. The important thing about the notes/documents collection is that it is the heart of the genealogist's research: it contains everything that is known about families and individuals of interest to the project.

This collection should also contain written narratives drawn from the memory of the researcher or his immediate family. These invaluable memories should be treated no differently than the documents collected. They should be written up on standard notepaper and incorporated into the collection. To bring all of these notes and documents together requires some work, and therefore some guidelines to follow in taking notes will make the work easier to manage.

## Basic Rules in Taking Notes

Here are four basic rules in taking notes for any genealogical project. These rules are based on standard historical research practices, but because of the special needs of genealogists, the rules apply specifically to family research techniques:

1. Control the sheet size
2. Separate sheets by surname
3. Separate surname sheets by the place of origin
4. Give every sheet a page number

Each of these four rules is explained below:

## 1. Control the Sheet Size

Nearly every student may have learned how to prepare for a written essay in high school by using 3" x 5" index cards, noting such things as the author's name, publisher, date of publication, etc., followed by a brief quote or two from the sources he or she had found in the library. This method worked well because the cards sorted easily and provided a bibliography once the report had been written.

However, genealogical researchers attempting to use this system will quickly discover that they rarely will have enough room on the card to write all the notes they want to capture. Not only that, genealogists are fond of copying whole pages of text from books, not just a few notes here and there. To make matters even worse, genealogists receive information from a variety of sources—letters from relatives, documents from vital statistics offices, interview notes, phone notes, or information from other genealogists. The nature of genealogical research does not allow the effective use of 3" x 5" cards, because a separate collection of the full-sized documents would then be necessary.

Genealogical researchers have also been known to go to the library without a note pad, using whatever paper they could beg, borrow, or steal to write down the latest census data they found. If the little sheet of paper is covered with a larger sheet of paper in the file box at home, the little sheet of paper will probably be in the "lost" category in the near future.

Standardizing the sheet size using 8½" x 11" paper solves this problem. If every note is taken on this sheet size, the notes can be well organized at the time they are created. The little pieces of paper can be taped to standard sheets to bring them into conformity, and if a researcher follows this simple rule faithfully, the ability to find notes and documents for later analysis will be enhanced immediately. Genealogists can adapt the 3" x 5" system into an 8½" x 11" system quite easily. The rewards are great.

To make this technique even better, use a pre-printed form to take all notes. This has several advantages. First, the sheet size will be controlled at the time the note is taken. Three-hole paper saves having to punch holes later, and the sheet has a place to be filed when taken home. An example of such a form for genealogical note-taking is shown on page 10.

## 2. Separate Sheets by Surname

Many genealogists are already separating documents by the surname of the family to which they pertain. A "surname book," that is, a standard three-hole notebook, is commonly used by genealogists to contain everything that is known about one surname, including those people who married into the family or the collateral families to the main surname. At this level of collection, it is not neces-

# Reference
## Family Data Sheet

| SURNAME | *DOLLARHIDE* | RFDS NUMBER | *CA 127* |
|---|---|---|---|

Sheet *6* of *8*

Date: *11/2/87*  Researcher: *Wm Dollarhide*

**The following data was taken from a single source exactly as it was found.**

**Source of data**

☒ Book ☐ Periodical ☐ Film ☐ Other*  Author/Editor: *W.M. Weekley & H.H. Fout*

Title/Article: *"OUR HEROS, or United Brethern Home Missionaries"*

In/By *United Brethern in Christ*  Vol.  No.  Page *276* Pub. *1900 (?) Dayton, OH*

Data was obtained from the following: ☐ Library research ☒ Correspondence** ☐ Field research ☐ Oral dictation ☐ Fam. rec'ds ☐ Other*

**Census only**

☐ Soundex ☐ Schedules ☐ Mortality ☐ Printed ☐ Microfilm | Roll No. | Page | Fam. No.

| Year | State | County | Township | Subdistrict |
|---|---|---|---|---|

*California — 1860's*

### Our Heroes, or

"Revs. Alexander, Musselman, and William Dresser were solemnly ordained to the office of elder after the morning sermon on Sabbath, September 14, by the Bishop *pro tem.*, assisted by Revs. J. Dollarhide and B. B. Allen."

Mr. Sloan was appointed to a distant charge. In a letter to the Telescope shortly after conference, he said, "It falls to my lot to go to Humboldt Bay, a distance of three hundred and forty miles from Sacramento across the Coast Range Mountains." He might have sent some one else to this far-off mission, and himself remained where the work would have been less vexing, and the surroundings more congenial, but it was not like the hero to do so. He chose for himself the hardest field.

The moving of his family and goods was a great undertaking in view of the mountains to be crossed, and the lack of transportation facilities. Mrs. Sloan describes the journey most graphically in a recent communication: "We shipped our goods by steamer to Humboldt, and ourselves went over the mountains. The trip was hard and dangerous. When we struck the mountains proper the wagon-road ran out, and the balance of the way, one hundred and fifty miles, had to be made on horseback, with dangers besetting us on every hand. The Indians were on the warpath and doing their most bloody work. We found that an escort of armed men was necessary, which it took some time to provide for. During the entire journey we had been camping

**Long, Dangerous Move** *(marginal side-note)*

276

*← this is Rev. John Dollarhide. He went to Calif. in 1860 — became circuit rider for U.B. church.*

*Rev. Israel Sloan was husband of Mrs. Sloan mentioned here.*

*Rev. J. Dollarhide named a son Israel Sloan Dollarhide, so he must have been a close friend.*

*Other Information:  ☒ Indexed

**From *Photocopy rec'd from Ione Conrd SMITH, 22026 Riverside Dr, Elkhorn, NE 68022 From United Brethern archives.*

sary to separate known ancestors from "suspected" ancestors. The important thing is that the person has the right surname and could be important to the project.

As the notes are gathered, write the surname at the top of the page and devote that page only to the surname or names connected with that surname.

Typically, genealogists find themselves sitting in front of a microfilm projector copying down notes from original records. Even if the genealogist was careful to copy all of the Johnson family records from one county, what happens sometimes is that another surname besides Johnson pops up—something that was not expected. This happens frequently in the course of collecting genealogical records. The serious mistake is to mix these surnames on the same sheet of paper. If the Brown family is on the same sheet as the Johnson family, even though those two families were not related to each other, the only recourse later might be to use a pair of scissors to get the notes separated by the surname. Therefore, simply turning the page when another surname is found will separate the surnames as the notes are taken.

Separating documents into surname books limits what is stored in the books to just the notes and documents and does not admit such things as lists of libraries, genealogical societies, or other material not directly related to a certain surname. The goal is to create a collection of reference material relating to a certain surname in such a way that family sheets can be prepared later—but with assurances that all of the known facts are easy to find.

A family record mentioning several other surnames that married into the family could all be saved as part of the main surname. The surname book contains information about the families and individuals important to the project, not necessarily just the known relatives. This is a key element in storing references in this manner. The problem of what to do with non-relatives has been solved: treat them the same as the relatives at this level of collection. If later research reveals that a reference item is not part of the family at all, the sheet can be removed and discarded. But until that time, the collection can contain any and all references to the surname of interest to the project.

Now the rules begin to make sense. If the same sheet size is used—3-hole, 8½" x 11" notepaper—and all surnames are separated on different sheets, a system of collecting notes will begin to pay off. With these two rules only, the note does not need to be stacked on top of the pile at home—any new sheet can immediately go into a surname book as another page.

## 3. Separate Surname Sheets by the Place of Origin

Once the documents have been stored on the same sheet size and placed in the appropriate book for the surname, the next step is to break down the sheets by the place, or origin, of the record to be saved. The logic behind this concept needs to be explained. There are three vital pieces of information every genealogist must know to pursue genealogical evidence: (1) a name, (2) a date, and (3) a place. With these three things known, a treasure chest of information will be made available for further research. Of these three, the *place* is the one that tells you *where* to look for further information. The place of the event, such as the birth, death, marriage, residence, etc., is what a genealogist *must* know before a copy of that record can be obtained.

We live in a record-keeping society. The jurisdiction that created the record is the *place*. That jurisdiction must be known before we can learn anything. If this fact is clear, then the idea of separating source material by the place is a logical step to take. Therefore, the many sheets of notes and documents pertaining to one family surname can be further separated by the origin of the records. Experienced genealogists know that once the county of residence has been established, a wealth of information awaits in the courthouse, the local library, the funeral homes, the cemeteries, the local genealogical societies, etc., all of which can provide much important information about a family that lived in the locality. That information cannot be found without first knowing *where* to look.

Separating the sheets by the place is an easy task to control because nearly every single genealogical reference item can have a place attached to it. So, the top of the sheet should first show the surname for the record, followed by some designator of the place of origin.

For example, the surname book could contain all of the Johnsons in Iowa in one section and the Ohio Johnsons in another section. If the Johnson family of interest started out with an immigrant to New Jersey, followed by migrations later to Ohio, then Indiana, then Iowa, etc., these state sections could be arranged in that particular order—which would tend to put the family reference material in a loose chronological order for the time periods they were in a particular state.

The place designation can be broken down further. If there were many Johnsons in Ohio, it may be worthwhile to separate this section by county. The important thing about this method of organizing notes is that when a new piece of information about the Johnson family in Ohio is found, the genealogist knows where to look for what is known about the family in that area. It should be easy to determine if the information is something repeated or is indeed new information.

The Reference Family Data Sheet example on page 10 indicates how a *surname/place* designator can be used. A two-letter code commonly used by the U.S. Postal Service is an effective way of giving a place designation. When the note is first being prepared, write the surname at the top of the page, then the place designator. The pre-printed form, of course, gives the genealogist a reminder of what needs to be done for every note and document prepared.

## 4. Give Every Sheet a Page Number

The fourth rule is simply to give every page a number. With the surname notebook organized in sections by place of origin, each sheet can be given a number that allows for the retrieval and return of sheets to a proper position. A sheet number need only be a consecutive number starting with number 1, adding numbers as sheets are accumulated.

The full sheet number might be Johnson/OH/24, meaning the sheet belongs in the Johnson surname book in the

Ohio section, and within that section it is page 24. This sheet number is assigned on a "first-come, first-served" basis, so there is no need to rearrange sheets later to get 1790 records before 1870 records. Genealogists find and collect records in random order, so they can be filed randomly too. This allows for adding sheets within a section as records are found.

But, since the references have already been sorted by surname/place, the sheet number is simply a designator to put a sheet back into a known position, and it provides the means of *indexing* reference sheets later. The page number is a key element in this filing system. If an index is to be prepared in the future, or if the genealogist plans to use a computer someday, page numbers will be critically important.

## Review of the Four Steps

Using four simple rules a genealogist can organize his notes and documents in a retrievable form: First, control the sheet size by using standard 8 1/2" x 11" paper for taking notes. The use of a pre-printed form like the Reference Family Data Sheet simplifies this step. A plain sheet of paper works too, but having a pre-printed form helps in keeping the citations for the sources consistent. The form also acts as a reminder of good record-keeping practices. Capturing the full source citation is essential if anyone is to review the work later.

Second, separate sheets by the surname of interest. If more than one surname is discussed, additional copies can be made and stored with the appropriate surname book. The surname is a critical and logical factor in finding records later.

Sorting the records by surname makes sense because as new information is found, the surname book is the first place to check to see if the new information adds critical data or is just a repeat of items already collected

Third, create a surname notebook to store the sheets, and divide the book into sections for the place of origin of the records. If there are many records for a certain place, the group can be further broken down by the county or even the city. Since the *place* is so critical in finding records, this is a logical way to store the records and documents.

Fourth, and finally, give every sheet a number so an index to the records can be made later. This important step also allows for a sheet to be removed from the notebook, compared with other sheets, and returned to a known place in the book. Page numbers can be assigned as they are found, on a "first-come, first-served" basis.

## Summary

The most serious problems in collecting reference material for a genealogical project can be solved if some basic rules are followed. Controlling the sheet size, separating surnames, separating sheets by the place of origin, and giving every sheet a page number will maintain the order required to retrieve records instantly and compare them with others. A standard, pre-printed form will make this method of collecting material easier to control.

All of these concepts can be applied further, because having such a well-organized reference collection will allow for the project to move in any direction the genealogist chooses. Creating family sheets from the individual reference sheets is the next step, and in the following section the use of the reference collection will prove why this part of the research project is the most important of all. If the full details about the people being researched cannot be found quickly, the whole system falls apart.

❀    ❀    ❀    ❀    ❀

# Section 3

# Retrieving Notes and Compiling Family Sheets

## Introduction

If the notes and documents are organized as described in Section 2, a genealogist has the means of locating multiple sheets for analysis. The process of comparing and compiling information from notes is one which most experienced genealogists understand. However, the problem of locating every research item can be frustrating if the notes are not in a place where they can be removed (or returned) easily.

The next step of compiling a family sheet is the point where most genealogists compare the notes, evaluating the contradictions that always occur, and then make a decision about the dates, places, and events necessary to enter information about the family members. This process is sometimes lengthy and worrisome, and often leads to ideas of where new research may be necessary. With a large collection of research notes, the process is even more complicated, and some means of indexing the information becomes critical.

With the notes and documents easily retrieved from the surname notebooks, a family sheet can be prepared more easily, but more importantly, a complete list of every sheet that was used to compile the family information can be cited.

## The Importance of Genealogical Evidence

Genealogists have at their disposal a rule of law called the Preponderance of Evidence. It is possible—if one can fully document all sources—to make assertions about the relationships between people. There may not be a single document that states, "He was the son of . . ." in your document files, but there may be overwhelming evidence to demonstrate that a relationship of father to son was indeed the case. If a court of law in the U.S. can accept such evidence, then it can be used by genealogists as well.

In fact, there are numerous instances in which professional genealogists have testified in court about the genealogical evidence regarding an heir to property, or some other matter in which genealogical evidence was in question. Genealogical evidence is no different from the evidence provided in a criminal case, where the prosecuting attorney must produce overwhelming evidence that the accused was indeed the criminal. However, the important fact about evidence is that *everyone* who reviews it must come to the same conclusion. Therefore, the pieces of evidence must be made available so that anyone can scrutinize the findings. If the same conclusion is reached, then it is indeed possible to make an assertion about "the son of . . ." without having a single document that actually states that fact.

Any reference to a person, however slight, should be included in the notes/documents collection. This means, for instance, that an obituary should be obtained even if the death certificate for this person has already been acquired. It also means that any other piece of evidence relating to that death should be gathered, e.g., survivors' memories, funeral programs, cemetery office records, tombstone inscriptions, stone mason records, insurance papers, social security records, and anything that may give clues about the survivors of the deceased. The more references collected, the more information will be revealed about ancestors or descendants of the person who died.

Genealogists who do not follow these basic principles are the ones who wonder why they cannot find further information about their ancestors. It may be a cliché, but the rule should be "never leave a stone unturned." And these items—some revealing vital statistics, others revealing only tid-bits of information about a person—are the items that receive attention

in the note-gathering phase of the project. With all the pieces brought together, perhaps by placing the sheets side-by-side, the evaluation process begins. Eventually, a family may take shape.

# Preparing a List for a Family Sheet

There are several ways of listing the sources and itemizing the evidence for genealogical purposes. First, a genealogist could simply write a narrative that describes the steps taken, listing every source and the conclusions reached. Second, a formal list could be prepared that itemizes all sources that make any mention of one person, regardless of the nature of the source. And third, such a list could be prepared for each family group, showing the page number in the notes/documents collection where the information is found.

This latter method has merit if the family sheet is being prepared anyway: Why not simply list every reference item that was used to compile the family information? Better yet, why not use the back side of the family sheet to do it? This is good record-keeping, because in compiling the family sheet every reference item from the documents file can be listed one at a time. Then, as new information is added, the new reference item can be added to the list as well.

Remember that the suggestion was for every reference sheet to have a number—now the importance of that page number is evident. But beyond the simple reference to the page, more informa-

# Compiled
## Family Data Sheet

Compiled By: *Wm. Dollarhide*     Updated: *3/1/88*

| CFDS NUMBER | 16/17 |
|---|---|

This sheet is a composite of **28** REFERENCE Family Data Sheets, which are itemized on the reverse side of this sheet.

| HUSBAND | ID No. 16 | Full Name JESSE DOLLARHIDE | DATE OF BIRTH | day month year *abt 1785* |
|---|---|---|---|---|

Other Names or Nicknames

Physical Description

child of    children. No. of brothers    No. of sisters

Other details

PLACE OF BIRTH — Town / Township / County *Prob. Randolph* / State/Country *No. Carolina*

**HIS DEATH**
Date of death *22 Feb 1840* Cause _____ Died at the age of ___ years. ___ months. ___ days
Place of death *Tippecanoe Co Indiana*
Mortuary / Cemetery

HIS FATHER *Prob. Hezekiah DOLLARHIDE* born *abt 1745* died *abt 1835*   CFDS NO. —
HIS MOTHER *Unknown* born ___ died ___

**MARRIAGE DATA**
Marriage recorded in Book *A* Page *128* of the County of *Preble Co*   State of *Ohio*
☐ Church record    ☐ Bible record    DATE OF MARRIAGE: *11 Nov. 1813*
Place of ceremony *in Preble Co OH*
Performed by *David PURVIANCE, Minister*
His other marriage(s) —
Her other marriage(s) *Mr. WILBUR*

| WIFE | ID No. 17 | Full Maiden Name NANCY PIERSON | DATE OF BIRTH | day month year *ca 1791* |
|---|---|---|---|---|

Other Names or Nicknames *PEARSON / Nancy Jane (?)*

Physical Description

child of    children. No. of brothers    No. of sisters

Other details

PLACE OF BIRTH — Town / Township / County / State/Country *KY or NC*

**HER DEATH**
Date of death *5 Feb. 1879* Cause *old age* Died at the age of *88* years. ___ months. ___ days
Place of death *Council Bluffs, Pottawattamie, Iowa*
Mortuary / Cemetery *Fairview Cem., Council Bluffs, IA*

HER FATHER *prob: Thomas PIERSON* born — died —   CFDS NO. —
HER MOTHER *prob: Nancy* ___ born — died —

| Children (Given Names) | b: Birth Date / m: Marriage Date / d: Death Date | PLACE OF EVENT | SPOUSE | CFDS NO. |
|---|---|---|---|---|
| 1 John (MY ANCESTOR #8) | b 1 Nov 1814 / m 3 Mar 1836 / d 22 Dec 1869 | Harrison Twp., Wayne Co IN / near Battleground, Tippecanoe Co IN / near Lodi, Calif. | Lucy REYNOLDS (MY ANCESTOR #9) | 8/9 |
| 2 Jesse Jr. | b 22 Aug 1816 / m 2 Jun 1836 / d 20 Aug 1888 | Wayne Co IN / Tippecanoe Co IN / Ashland, Jackson Co OR | Nancy MURPHEY | 8.2 |
| 3 William | b Aug 1820 / m 30 Aug 1843 / d 22 Sep 1904 | Wayne Co IN / Fountain Co IN / Roseburg, Douglas Co OR | Elvira DILL | 8.3 |
| 4 Elizabeth | b obt 1822 / m 19 Dec 1839 / d 20 Nov 1843 | Wayne Co IN / Tippecanoe Co IN / prob: Jasper Co IN | Preston McCORKEL | — |
| 5 Mary | b abt 1824 / m no further information / d | Wayne Co (?) IN | Mr. BRIDGES (?) | — |
| 6 Joel Haven | b 25 Jun 1827 / m 1848 / d 9 Oct 1878 | prob: Tippecanoe Co IN / prob: Jasper Co IN / Council Bluffs, IA. | Sarah Ann MEREDITH | 8.6 |
| 7 | b / m / d | | | |
| 8 | b / m / d | | | |

## Continuation of CFDS No. _16/17_

| Children (Given Names) | b: m: d: | Birth Date Marriage Date Death Date | PLACE OF EVENT | SPOUSE | CFDS NO. |
|---|---|---|---|---|---|
| 9 | b | | | | |
| | m | | | | |
| | d | | | | |
| 10 | b | | | | |
| | m | | | | |
| | d | | | | |
| 11 | b | | | | |
| | m | | | | |
| | d | | | | |
| 12 | b | | | | |
| | m | | | | |
| | d | | | | |
| 13 | b | | | | |
| | m | | | | |
| | d | | | | |
| 14 | b | | | | |
| | m | | | | |
| | d | | | | |

The following is a list of all source material concerning this family which has been found to date. For full details, refer to the REFERENCE Family Data Sheets (RFDS) itemized below. Each RFDS is filed by surname, place and sheet number.

| Item No. | Reference Family Data Sheet Surname | State/No. | Type of Record | In Reference to | Information Given |
|---|---|---|---|---|---|
| 1 | DOLLARHIDE | IN 3 | History | Jesse Sr. | Mentioned (1830s) |
| 2 | " | IN 11 | 1840 census | John | living in Jasper Co IN |
| 3 | " | IN 13 | 1840 census | Jesse Jr. | Includes Nancy & family |
| 4 | " | IN 20 | Land Rec'ds | Jesse Sr. | Deeds, etc., Wayne Co IN |
| 5 | " | IN 21 | Marriage | William | 1843, Fountain Co IN |
| 6 | " | IN 22 | Estate papers | Jesse Sr. | 1840, Tippecanoe Co IN |
| 7 | " | IN 23 | " " | " " | w/family listed |
| 8 | " | IN 25 | " " | " " | Sale notes |
| 9 | " | IN 26 | " " | " " | Admin. Records of sales |
| 10 | " | IN 27 | 1830 census | Jesse Sr. | living Fountain Co IN |
| 11 | " | IN 42 | 1850 census | John/Wm. | Families listed, Jasper Co IN |
| 12 | " | IN 43 | 1850 census | Joel/Jesse Jr | " " " " |
| 13 | " | IN 45 | 1820 census | Jesse Sr. | Wayne Co, next to Hezekiah |
| 14 | " | IN 47 | Appraisal-estate | " " | Itemized list of property |
| 15 | " | IN 48 | Indebture | " " | Mortaged land |
| 16 | " | IN 49 | Bill in chancery | " " | lists heirs of Jesse Sr. |
| 17 | " | IN 50 | " " " | " " | " " " " |
| 18 | " | IN 51 | Summons | " " | heirs to appear in court |
| 19 | " | IN 52 | Marriage | Elizabeth | Tippecanoe Co IN 1839 |
| 20 | " | IN 53 | " | Jesse Jr. | " " 1836 |
| 21 | " | IN 54 | " | John | " " 1836 |
| 22 | " | IN 61 | Probate papers | Jesse Sr. | Admin. estate of Thos. PIERSON |
| 23 | " | IN 62 | land atlas | " " | lamd in Wayne Co IN 1820s |
| 24 | " | IN 71 | Deeds | John/Jesse Jr. | land sales, Jasper Co IN |
| 25 | " | OH 23 | Marriage | Jesse Sr. | to Nancy PIERSON, 1813 |
| 26 | PIERSON | IN 2 | 1820 census | Thomas | lived near Jesse/Nancy |
| 27 | " | IN 4 | Guardianship | Nancy/Jesse | Chi of Thomas PIERSON |
| 28 | " | IN 5 | " | " " | Nancy "LONGACRE" |

tion might be worthwhile having in the list. Here is an example of how this system works, using a family sheet designed to list the references.

The sample of a COMPILED Family Data Sheet on pages 17 and 18 demonstrates how this method works. The front of the sheet is a standard group sheet for a family, giving the husband, wife, and children with their pertinent genealogical data. The back side of the sheet has a place to list every REFERENCE Family Data Sheet that was used for that particular family.

Note that the first thing needed is to tell the genealogist which surname book the item came from, what section within the surname book, and what page number within that section. "Dollarhide/IN/3" indicates that the reference is in the Dollarhide surname book in the Indiana section, and within that section it is page 3.

There are several advantages in listing all references on the family sheet in this way. Not only does the list keep track for the genealogist of every research item that was used to compile the family, it also can be mailed to other genealogists showing what has been collected for that family. Genealogists who receive letters from other genealogists asking for "everything you have on the Brown family" can send the list of references first.

The list also tells the genealogist where to find records that could have been stored in more than one place. For example, records concerning Nancy Pierson before her marriage can be stored with the Pierson surname book. Records after her marriage to Jesse Dollarhide can be stored in the Dollar-hide surname book. A copy need not be made for each book if the list indicates where each particular reference has been filed.

## Listing References for One Person

Another optional step in compiling information is to make a sheet for each pedigree ancestor. A special form to do this, called a Master Data Sheet, is shown for Mary Winslow. (See page 20.) The concept of having one sheet for all of the vital statistics for one person is one which many genealogists find useful. This particular form has expanded the information about one person and includes a small pedigree chart to assign an ahnentafel number to each pedigree ancestor. (Ahnentafel numbers are described in detail in Section 4.)

On the back side of the Master Data Sheet is another form called a Research Log. This lists every Reference Family Data Sheet that mentions Mary Winslow. It is a similar list to the one on the Compiled Family Data Sheet and may contain the same information. The advantage of this is that it enables you to locate each item for one person and then prepare the master vital statistics for that person.

## Itemizing Events

Many genealogists have developed indexing methods similar to the lists on the family sheets or individual sheets, but expanding the information so that one entry is one event. One of the most practical methods is to prepare 3" x 5" index cards for each person and event, with a citation to the source.

# Master Data Sheet
**For One Pedigree Ancestor**

| NAME | Mary WINSLOW | ANCESTOR NUMBER | 27 |
|---|---|---|---|

Researcher: *Wm. Dollarhide*

The following information concerns one person – a pedigree ancestor. Refer to Research Log for this person for an itemized list of sources. See Family Group sheet for details concerning this person's spouse, children, and all family births, deaths and marriages.

| FULL NAME AT TIME OF BIRTH | Mary WINSLOW | BIRTH DATE | 24 day   Jan. month   1824 year |
|---|---|---|---|

Other names, including nicknames:

Physical description:

2nd Child of 8 children.  Number of brothers: 5   Number of sisters: 2

Church records: NC & IN Quaker Reads. Much family info given.

| PLACE OF BIRTH | Town/City near 'Back Creek' |
| | Township |
| | County Randolph |
| | State/Country No. Carolina |

**MARRIAGE DATA**

Name of spouse: John NEEDHAM      Ancestor No. 26

Married at: Grant Co Indiana

1 of 1 marriages.  Date of license: 31 Oct 1843      Date of ceremony: 2 Nov 1843

Marriage performed by: Solomon PARSON      Title: J.P.

Witnesses:

Names of children of above marriage: Marion, Susan, Josiah, Jerome, Robert, Margaret, Oliver, and Mary NEEDHAM

Other marriages: None

**DEATH**

Date of death 21 Nov 1915      cause Old age      at age of 92 years, 10 months, 11 days

Place of death / burial: Galt, Sacramento Co CA

Undertaker / cemetery: Galt Cemetery (Formerly I.O.O.F)

**PROBATE**

Jurisdiction: None

Disposition: None

**REMARKS**

Mary WINSLOW was born and raised a Quaker. However, when she was married to John NEEDHAM, a non-Quaker, in a civil ceremony, she was "disowned" from the Quakers. Most of her children were raised in Grant Co IN. The family moved to Union Co IA in 1850s. She lived with her husband near Shenandoah, IA until his death in 1905. Soon after, she went to live with a grand-son in California.

- 27. Mary WINSLOW
  - 54. John WINSLOW
    - 108. Henry WINSLOW
      - 216. Thomas WINSLOW
      - 217. Elizabeth PHELPS
    - 109. Elizabeth NEEDHAM
      - 218. —— NEEDHAM
      - 219. Unknown
  - 55. Elizabeth HENLEY
    - 110. Jesse HENLEY
      - 220. John HENLEY
      - 221. Mary ALBERTSON (?)
    - 111. Miriam BUNDY
      - 222. Jehu BUNDY
      - 223. Lydia GRIFFIN

# Research Log
## For One Pedigree Ancestor

| NAME | Mary WINSLOW | ANCESTOR NUMBER | 27 |
|------|--------------|------------------|-----|

Researcher: *Wm. Dollarhide*

The following data represents every research item that has been found about one person.

| LOG NO. | Reference Family Data Sheet Surname | State/No | Type of Record | Information Given |
|---------|--------------|----------|----------------|-------------------|
| 1 | WINSLOW | NC 1 | Quaker Rec'ds | birth, death, marriage, parents |
| 2 | " | IN 5 | Marriage Rec'd | for Mary W. & John NEEDHAM |
| 3 | NEEDHAM | IA 3 | Family Bible | NEEDHAM Family. Gives birth, marriage |
| 4 | WINSLOW | IN 6 | Quaker Rec'ds | Mary w/ Parents in Randolph Co NC. birthdate. |
| 5 | " | IN 7 | " " " | Mary mentioned. Member |
| 6 | " | NC 11 | Family History | by L.K. WILLIAMS. Includes WINSLOW/NEEDHAM |
| 7 | NEEDHAM | IA 4 | Family Bible | NEEDHAM family: all vital statistics given |
| 8 | " | IA 5 | Bio. Sketch | For son, Josiah. Mary mentioned |
| 9 | " | IA 6 | 1870 Census | NEEDHAM family. Mary, John & ch. |
| 10 | " | IA 7 | 1880 Census | " " " |
| 11 | " | IA 8 | 1900 Census | " " . Living alone w. John |
| 12 | " | IN 2 | Marr. Rec'd | John & Mary (same as WINSLOW IN 5) |
| 13 | " | IN 3 | Quaker Rec'ds | Mentions Mary |
| 14 | " | IN 4 | Marr. Rec'd | John & Mary. From Grant Co Courthouse. |
| 15 | " | IN 5 | 1850 Census | NEEDHAM family. Mary, John & ch. |
| 16 | NEEDHAM | IN 11 | Obituary | For Mary (WINSLOW) NEEDHAM d. 1915 in CA. |

All genealogical events can be reduced to four basic categories: a birth, a marriage, a death, or a residence. Obviously, there are many more events than these, but these four categories will identify all genealogical events. A residence event is one in which the reference item does not indicate a birth, marriage, or death, but rather a tax list, a deed, a will, a census, etc. These "proof of residence" references can be grouped together as "residence" events. If a 3" x 5" card is prepared for each event it may appear as shown below:

3" x 5" CARD (EVENT) INDEX:

Surname: WINSLOW Ref. Source: IN 6
Given: Mary ID: 27
Event/Date: b 1824
Place of Event: Randolph Co NC
Type of Record: Quaker Recds
Remarks: Mary was dau of John and
Elizabeth (Henley) Winslow

The above card entry is for one person, one date, one place, and one event. If this was a marriage record, another card would be made for the other marriage partner. The idea is to have all the events segregated so that they can be sorted either by name, by place, or by date.

The advantage to the 3" x 5" card index is that the names and events can be entered into a computer database easily. A computer provides a potential sorting capability unmatched by humans, but for the computer to be used as an effective tool, the entries must be logically prepared. An "event-oriented" database is the easiest type of system to convert to a computer system later. For example, each

of the events from the cards could be transferred to a computer file, with each card being one "record." See Section 6 for more detailed information about such a computer database.

## Summary

Section 1 described the differences between a pedigree, lineage, and descendancy. The next section detailed a method of controlling the notes and documents using surname books, standardizing the sheet size, separating by surname and place, and giving every sheet a page number. Section 3 included a description of various methods of indexing the events, names, places, and dates from the notes/documents file. Family sheets and individual sheets (such as the Master Data Sheet), each having a place to itemize the sources used, were also described.

An index to the documentation merely makes reference to it. The heart of the research collection is the documents themselves, and these should be easily retrievable so that good judgments can be made when compiling family sheets, individual sheets, or later presentations of the facts for a genealogical project. An index is impossible without giving every sheet in the documents file a page number.

But what about organizing the family sheets? Genealogists may have accumulated stacks of these sheets over a period of time, and some good record-keeping practices can be followed here as well. In the next section some important suggestions will be made to solve this problem.

❁   ❁   ❁   ❁   ❁

# Section 4

# Ahnentafel Numbering

## Introduction

Ahnentafel numbering relates to a pedigree. The German word "ahnentafel" —meaning "ancestor table"—however, implies that the numbers on the pedigree chart are not repeated, but continue to rise. Ahnentafel numbers allow each ancestor in the pedigree to have a discrete identification number, and there are many advantages to this method of ancestor numbering.

Unfortunately, some genealogists are not using ahnentafel numbers because most of the printed pedigree charts available do not allow their use without modifying the pre-printed numbers on the charts. To explain this problem, and to show how ahnentafel numbers can be used, a brief review of a pedigree and a comparison of two numbering methods is shown below.

## Pedigree—A Review

A pedigree is an identification of all direct ancestors for a person. A pedigree chart diagrams these ancestors, moving *backward* in time. Pedigree numbers appear on the following chart:

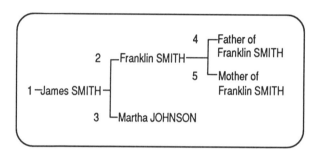

In the example above, James SMITH starts the pedigree. As the first person, his pedigree number is number 1 (pedigree number 1 can be male or female). For every generation thereafter the male should always be in the *upper* position and have an *even* number. The father of Franklin SMITH can be determined by a simple rule: The father of any person is double that person's number. So Franklin SMITH's father would be number 4.

To find the mother of Franklin SMITH, the rule is to double the person's number and ADD 1. Therefore, the mother of Franklin SMITH would be number 5.

These numbers can be continued indefinitely. However, many genealogists use pedigree forms that already have the first several generations pre-printed. To continue onto another sheet, the number for each person changes—and this be-

23

comes very confusing if some reference is not made to the chart number for cross-referencing. This method of numbering continuation sheets for a pedigree chart is used by the Family History Library and many other publishers of printed forms. An example of "changing" pedigree numbers is shown below:

**METHOD 1: Pedigree Charts WITHOUT ahnentafel numbering extended**

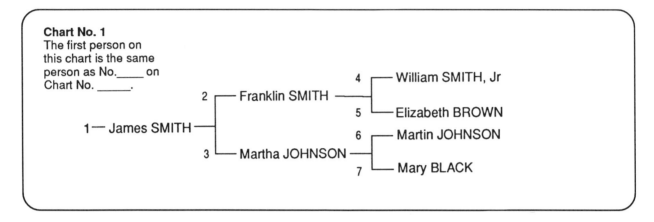

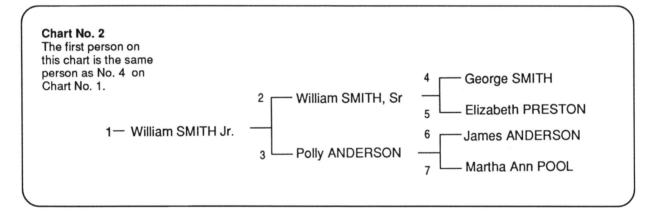

In the above examples, each chart starts with number 1, but that person is cross-referenced to the previous chart on which he/she appears. Every new chart starts with number 1 again. This method causes ancestors to have a different number on more than one chart, hence the need for keeping cross-referenced notes on every chart. Genealogists using this method have lost any chance of using the pedigree numbers as identification numbers. In order to give each person a unique number, another set of numbers would have to be assigned.

Ahnentafel numbers, on the other hand, enable the genealogist to look at the pedigree from many different perspectives. They allow him several ways of organizing the ancestors other than the standard pedigree diagram, while still maintaining control of "who is who."

An example of ahnentafel numbering
is shown below:

**METHOD 2: Pedigree Charts with ahnentafel numbering extended**

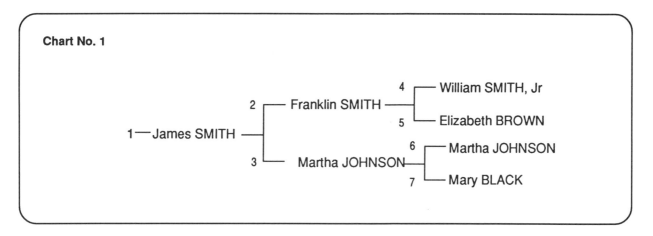

**Chart No. 1**

1—James SMITH
2 — Franklin SMITH
3 — Martha JOHNSON
4 — William SMITH, Jr
5 — Elizabeth BROWN
6 — Martha JOHNSON
7 — Mary BLACK

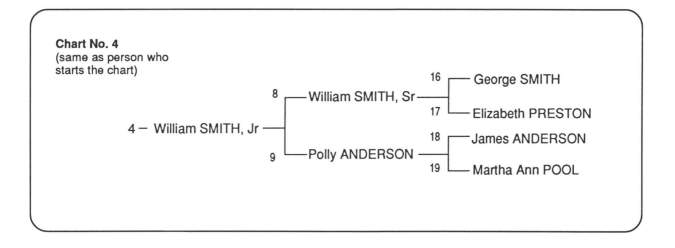

**Chart No. 4**
(same as person who
starts the chart)

4 — William SMITH, Jr
8 — William SMITH, Sr
9 — Polly ANDERSON
16 — George SMITH
17 — Elizabeth PRESTON
18 — James ANDERSON
19 — Martha Ann POOL

In the above examples, William SMITH, Jr. appears on both charts, but his number does not change. This is a method of continuing ahnentafel numbering, and each person then has a discrete ID number which can be used for filing purposes.

Any person in the last generation shown could be the first person on another chart, and by doubling that number, the number of his/her father is already known. Using number 19, Martha Ann POOL, as an example, we get the following:

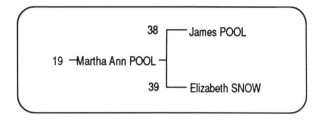

The father of 38 would be 76, the mother of 38 would be 77. A wife is always one number higher than her husband. This simple rule means that any person's number can be determined in advance, even if the name is not known.

Changing to this system will give the genealogist some very useful planning tools. For example, the Germans have taken the rules from the diagram and then displayed the ahnentafel as a ladder:

| | | |
|---|---|---|
| 1. | James SMITH, Jr. | Generation I |
| 2. | Franklin SMITH, Sr. | Generation II |
| 3. | Martha JOHNSON | " |
| 4. | William SMITH, Jr. | Generation III |
| 5. | Elizabeth BROWN | " |
| 6. | Martin JOHNSON | " |
| 7. | Mary BLACK | " |
| 8. | William SMITH, Sr. | Generation IV |
| 9. | Polly ANDERSON | " |
| 10. | —— BROWN | " |
| 11. | —— —— | " |
| 12. | —— JOHNSON | " |
| 13. | —— —— | " |
| 14. | —— BLACK | " |
| 15. | —— —— | " |
| 16. | George SMITH | Generation V |
| 17. | Elizabeth PRESTON | " |
| 18. | James ANDERSON | " |
| 19. | Martha Ann POOL | " |
| — | | |
| — | | |
| 38. | James POOL | Generation VI |
| 39. | Elizabeth SNOW | " |

The preceding list is no different than a pedigree diagram, but the ancestors are listed in a table. Note that in this list certain names are omitted, and certain names were added where the surname could be predicted. For example, the father of any male can be predicted to have the same surname. Therefore, it was possible to predict that number 10 would be a BROWN, as was the case also for number 12, — JOHNSON, and number 14, — BLACK.

The simplicity of the ahnentafel is what makes it so practical. For example, the rule about all males having even numbers and all females having odd numbers gives the genealogist another list that can be very useful:

1. SMITH, James
3. JOHNSON, Martha
5. BROWN, Elizabeth
7. BLACK, Mary
9. ANDERSON, Polly

If the above list were continued—being all odd numbers—it would list every female in the pedigree. (Remember that number 1 is the only odd number that can be male or female.) But the list is also a listing of every different *surname* in the pedigree! This is true because every female brings a different surname to the pedigree.

SURNAME LIST:

1. SMITH
3. JOHNSON
5. BROWN
7. BLACK
9. ANDERSON

Simply by listing the odd numbers, every surname in the pedigree can be listed in numerical order. Such a list can help a genealogist understand the position of surnames in relation to number 1—the person who starts the pedigree. It is now possible to identify a surname as "my number 7 surname is BLACK," or "my number 9 surname is ANDERSON."

Behind each of these odd numbers is a male with the same surname. So a rearrangement of the ahnentafel allows another method of viewing a lineage on a pedigree chart—this time just for one surname. Compile a surname list by starting with any odd number, then double that number to find the father of that person, double again to continue:

```
  1. James SMITH
  2. Franklin SMITH
  4. William SMITH, Jr.
  8. William SMITH, Sr.
 16. George SMITH
 32. ——— SMITH
 64. ——— SMITH
128. ——— SMITH
256. ——— SMITH
     . . . and so on . . .
```

The same list could be prepared with all of the spouses to show all of the marriages into the SMITH line. For example:

```
 1. James SMITH
 2. Franklin SMITH ............... m 3. Martha JOHNSON
 4. William SMITH, Jr. .......... m 5. Elizabeth BROWN
 8. William SMITH, Sr. ......... m 9. Polly ANDERSON
16. George SMITH ............... m 17. Eliz. PRESTON
32. ——— SMITH ............... m 33. Name unknown
```

A special form to create a list such as the one above is shown on page 28. This form is called an Ancestor Table, and it gives a place to display the ahnentafel list for one surname as far as information is known—up to 12 generations on one page. This form is an example of how the

use of ahnentafel numbers gives the genealogist a completely different method of displaying the pedigree. More importantly, this simple form can cure an age-old problem genealogists have had with large, cumbersome pedigree charts.

Many genealogists have been using very large pedigree charts that fold out, with room to display 15 or more generations. There is nothing wrong with using these large charts, but after many times of folding and unfolding the chart begins to fall apart. It does not take long for the chart to become dog-eared, rumpled, and generally a mess to handle.

The Ancestor Table is the answer to this problem. This form can be bound into a booklet, with each sheet showing a different surname. The first page would be surname number 1, followed by separate pages for surname numbers 3, 5, 7, 9, and so on. With a sheet prepared for each surname, every ancestor in the pedigree will be listed twice—once with the main surname, and again with the spouse's surname. Such a booklet of 100 sheets will be 8½" x 11", and less than a half-inch thick. It is perfect for carrying in a briefcase or purse.

An Ancestor Table booklet has some other useful features as well. For example, by listing the surnames in numerical order, the first pages/surnames are those nearest to number 1 in the pedigree. A genealogist can use the booklet to ask what needs to be done on that surname before turning the page to the next surname. This acts as a reminder of work that may need to be done on a surname closer to number 1, and gives the genealogist some priority as to where work should be conducted first. This same process can be accomplished using

# Ancestor Table

| | |
|---|---|
| SURNAME | *DOLLARHIDE* |
| Ancestor Number | *1* |

Sheet *1* of *1*

Researcher *Wm. Dollarhide*

**◀■■■■ First Pedigree Ancestor with this Surname.**

**1** *William W. DOLLARHIDE*  — Married ▶ —  *Mary E. SMITH*
Father
Born *17 Apr 1942* Where *Seattle, King Co WA*  When *6 Oct 1967*
Died *—* Where *—*  Where *Carson City, NV*

**2** *Rev. Albert R. DOLLARHIDE* — Married ▶ **3** *Marjory W. WILES*
Grandfather
Born *19 Apr 1905* Where *Oakland, Douglas Co OR*  When *18 Jan 1930*
Died *18 Mar 1977* Where *Blaine, Whatcom Co WA*  Where *Puyallup, Pierce Co WA*

**4** *John C. DOLLARHIDE* — Married ▶ **5** *Addie McNAMER*
Born *17 Mar 1858* Where *Des Moines, Polk Co IA*  When *18 Sep 1887*
Died *7 Jun 1934* Where *Pt. Angeles, Clallam Co WA*  Where *Pittville, Shasta Co CA*

**8** *Rev. John DOLLARHIDE* — Married ▶ **9** *Lucy REYNOLDS*
Born *1 Nov 1814* Where *Wayne Co IN*  When *3 Mar 1836*
Died *22 Dec 1869* Where *near Lodi, San Juaquin Co CA*  Where *Tippecanoe Co IN*

**16** *Jesse DOLLARHIDE* — Married ▶ **17** *Nancy PIERSON*
Born *abt 1785* Where *prob: Randolph Co NC*  When *11 Nov 1813*
Died *22 Feb 1840* Where *Tippecanoe Co IN*  Where *Preble Co OH*

**32** *PROB: Hezekiah DOLLARHIDE* — Married ▶ **33** *— ? —*
Born *abt 1745* Where *prob: Randolph Co NC*  When *abt 1775-80*
Died *abt 1835* Where *Randolph Co IN*  Where *prob: Randolph Co NC*

**64** *Francis DOLLARHIDE (Jr.)* — Married ▶ **65** *Mary (——) BRADSHAW*
Born *ca 1700* Where *Baltimore Co MD*  When *abt 1723*
Died *ca 1779* Where *Randolph Co NC*  Where *Baltimore Co MD*

*(IMMIGRANT) to MD 1680:*
**128** *Francis DOLLAHYDE (Sr.)* — Married ▶ **129** *Providence TOLLEY*
Born *ca 1650* Where *British Isles (?)*  When *abt 1695*
Died *aft Oct 1721 / bet Jun 1722* Where *Baltimore Co MD*  Where *Ann Arrundell Co MD*

**256** *Unknown* — Married ▶
Born _____ Where _____  When _____
Died _____ Where _____  Where _____

— Married ▶
Born _____ Where _____  When _____
Died _____ Where _____  Where _____

— Married ▶
Born _____ Where _____  When _____
Died _____ Where _____  Where _____

— Married ▶
Born _____ Where _____  When _____
Died _____ Where _____  Where _____

a standard pedigree chart, but the advantage of having ahnentafel numbers is that they give a whole new arrangement of the ancestors, and thus a better understanding of the project in general.

# Ahnentafel Numbers on a Master Data Sheet

Section 3 described a special form called a Master Data Sheet (MDS) (see page 20). This form has several useful functions. First, it identifies each pedigree ancestor separately, and on the back side, the Research Log for that person gives a place to itemize every Reference Family Data Sheet that was used to collect information about that person. In addition, a small pedigree chart is provided to show the ahnentafel number for the person, plus four generations of the ancestry of that person.

Using an Ahnentafel Numbering System, this MDS form can be organized with the other pedigree ancestors in numerical order starting with numbers 1, 2, 3, 4, 5, 6, 7, and so on. The small pedigree chart acts as an index to the generations beyond, and the numbers themselves can be used to find a lineage in either direction, that is, the pedigree child or the ancestors.

This may be a complete departure from what most genealogists are doing, but this system of MDS forms filed numerically can organize a pedigree and provide the following in a logical format:

- Every person on a separate sheet
- A list of every reference item found for one person

- A place to compile the basic vital statistics for one person
- Notes and details not normally found on a family sheet.

In short, this form organizes the pedigree ancestors in a way that is simple and logical, yet provides instant access for further information. The MDS form does not replace a family sheet—it enhances the other compiled sheets to follow because it provides the first place to look for the direct ancestors in the pedigree project.

# Ahnentafel Numbers on a Family Sheet

Family sheets can be arranged by using the ahnentafel numbers for the husband and wife. Again, this may be a different way of organizing sheets for some genealogists, because the most common practice is to arrange sheets in alphabetical order, usually by the surname of the husband. There is nothing wrong with this technique, of course, but the ahnentafel system gives the genealogist a way of organizing these sheets by the numbers.

For example, to prepare a sheet for ancestor number 12 who married ancestor number 13, the family sheet could be identified as "Sheet No. 12/13." With all pedigree ancestor pairs appearing on family sheets, the numerical order for filing such sheets in a standard notebook might be shown as follows:

2/3
4/5
6/7
8/9
10/11
12/13
14/15
. . . and so on . . .

One of these sheets might appear as shown below:

```
12    Father
13    Mother
      1st child
      2nd child... (pedigree ancestor No. 6)
      3rd child
      4th child
```

Of course, pedigree ancestor number 6 could have been in any position—in this example that person was the 2nd child of number 12 and number 13. To find the pedigree child's number, divide the father's number in half. So in this case, the pedigree child has the number 6.

The siblings of number 6 can now be given a number too. These siblings are considered collateral lines to the main, direct pedigree ancestors, but a family sheet should include all of the children of the ancestors. Here is a suggested method:

```
12    Father
13    Mother
      1st child... 6.1
      2nd child... (pedigree ancestor No. 6)
      3rd child... 6.3
      4th child... 6.4
```

Adding a decimal acts as a flag. The decimal cancels the rule about odd for females and even for males. It also clearly indicates that the person is *not* a pedigree ancestor. The number to the right of the decimal is the birth order for that child. However, in the example given, since the pedigree child is whole number 6 and the 2nd child, the decimal 6.2 cannot be used. The pedigree child could have been in any birth order, including the 4th child position:

```
12    Father
13    Mother
      1st child... 6.1
      2nd child...6.2
      3rd child... 6.3
      4th child... 6 (pedigree ancestor No. 6)
```

Again, the use of ahnentafel numbers is what makes this numbering scheme possible. With these numbers a genealogist can identify the pedigree ancestors *and* the collateral lines and, with the ahnentafel number on the left, always know where the collateral person fits into the pedigree. The next section will give further details about identifying collateral lines, as well as their descendants.

## More on Ahnentafel Numbers

One of the first things a genealogist must do before starting the Ahnentafel Numbering System is to determine who will be number 1 on the pedigree. Number 1 is the person who starts the pedigree, and it could be said that the pedigree/ahnentafel "belongs" to that person. It is suggested that if a husband and wife are both working on their pedigree projects together that they make one of their children the first person, or number 1. This will place both the father and mother on the same pedigree as numbers 2 and 3.

For genealogists who have been using pre-printed pedigree forms and wish to change to the Ahnentafel Numbering System, it will be necessary to add the ahnentafel numbers to the existing charts. One technique is to add the ahnentafel numbers in parentheses above the pre-printed number already on the chart.

Another method, of course, would be to use a bottle of "white-out" to remove the pre-printed numbers and then write the ahnentafel numbers in by hand.

For example, if the continuation sheet begins with number 1, but the actual ahnentafel number should be 15, here is a method of doing this:

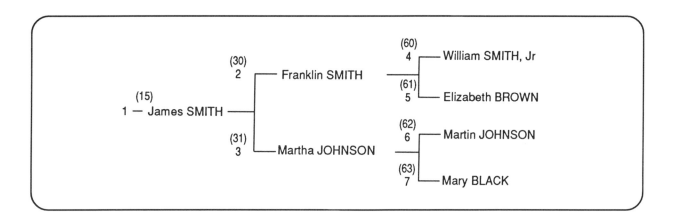

## Summary

The Ahnentafel Numbering System opens up a whole world of opportunity for genealogists. Special forms, special methods of displaying information, and a different way of looking at a pedigree project are all advantages that could not be enjoyed without utilizing this system. Pedigree ancestors can be organized in numerical order, and their individual vital statistic sheets and family sheets can also be filed in numerical order.

Collateral lines can be linked to the ahnentafel numbers as well, giving a complete numbering control for these persons.

The descendants of siblings can be identified using this system, but before taking this step any further, the next section will review genealogical numbering systems for a descendancy and a method of combining the ahnentafel numbers with the collateral numbers for any number of generations.

❁   ❁   ❁   ❁   ❁

# Section 5

# Descendancy Numbering

## Introduction

The Ahnentafel Numbering System works well for a pedigree, but for a descendancy a completely different numbering scheme is necessary. As explained in Section 1, the descendancy potentially identifies a much larger group of people than a pedigree. For such projects there are at least three accepted methods of assigning numbers to descendants, and all three need to be explained. The first method, called the Register System, is the standard used by national publications. Another system seen frequently in recent years is known as the Henry System. A method of combining ahnentafel numbers with the Henry System—a system developed by the author—will be explained shortly.

## The Register System

This descendancy numbering system was first used in the New England Historic Genealogical Society's periodical, *The New England Historical and Genealogical Register*—for short, the *Register*—hence the name of the system. As an example of the Register System in its purest form, the following partial descendancy was taken from a book published in 1984 by the Genealogical Publishing Company—*American Ancestors and Cousins of the Princess of Wales*, by Gary Boyd Roberts and William Addams Reitwiesner (extracted from page 92).

Descendants of Frank(lin H.) Work and of Ellen Wood [great-great-grandparents of The Princess of Wales]

1. FRANK(LIN H.) WORK, dry goods merchant, stockbroker, b. Chillicothe, Ohio, 10 Feb. 1819, d. New York, N.Y., 16 March 1911, son of John Wark and of Sarah Duncan Boude, m. New York, N.Y., 19 Feb. 1857, Ellen Wood, b. Chillicothe, Ohio, 18 July 1831, d. New York, N.Y., 22 Feb. 1877, dau. of John Wood and of Eleanor Strong.

Issue: (surname WORK):

2. a. Frances Eleanor, b. New York, N.Y., 27 Oct 1857, d. New York, N.Y., 26 Jan 1947.
3. b. George Paul, b. 8 Sept. 1858, d. Davos Platz, Kt. Grisons (Switz.), 25 Feb. 1900.
4. c. Lucy Bond, b. New York, N.Y., May 1860, d. New York, N.Y., 21 March 1934.

2. Frances Eleanor WORK, b. New York, N.Y., 27 Oct 1857, d. New York, N.Y., 26 Jan. 1947, m. (1) New York, N.Y., 22 Sept. 1880, div. Wilmington, Del., 3 March 1891,

James Boothby BURKE ROCHE, from 10 Sept., 1856, Hon. James Boothby BURKE ROCHE, from 1 Sept. 1920, 3rd Baron Fermoy, b. Twyford Abbey, Middx., 28 July 1851, d. Westminster, 30 Oct. 1920, son of Edmund BURKE ROCHE, 1st Baron Fermoy, and of Eliza Caroline BOOTHBY; m. (2) New York, N.Y., 4 Aug. 1905, div. New York, 5 Nov. 1909, as his second wife, Aurel BATONYI [he had m. (1) and div.], son of Leopold BATONYI.

Issue by first husband (surname BURKE ROCHE; styled from 1 Sept. 1920 "Hon."):

   a. Eileen, b. 1882, d. 1882
4. b. Cynthia, b. London, 10 Apr. 1884, d. Newport, R.I., 18 Dec 1966.
5. c. Edmund Maurice, b. Chelsea, 15 May 1885, [twin], d. King's Lynn, 8 July 1955.
   d. Francis George, b. Chelsea, 15 May 1885, [twin], d. Newport, R.I., 30 Oct 1958.

3. Lucy Bond WORK, b. New York, N.Y. May 1860, d. New York, N.Y., 21 March 1934, m. New York, N.Y., 27 Apr. 1887.

. . . . **more** . . . .

In the above example, the Register numbers are assigned with the first person as number 1, followed by his/her children as 2, 3, 4, etc. Not every person is assigned a number, however, only those whose line of descent will be continued later. Of the three children of Franklin Work, listed above as Frances, George, and Lucy, just two have been assigned numbers. Because George has no number assigned, we presume the author chose not to continue the descent-line of George Paul Work (which is the prerogative of the author).

There are two columns of information shown. The left margin indicates the "adult descent line," while the indented column indicates the children in their order of birth:

1. Franklin WORK
   2. a. Frances Eleanor WORK
      b. George Paul WORK
   3. c. Lucy Bond WORK

2. Frances Eleanor WORK

Except for the first progenitor, every person given a number will appear first as a child, the number indicating his/her position in the adult descent line. If no number is given, that will be the last time that child will be mentioned in the descendancy.

In the child column, brief vitals are listed. But in the adult column, more detail about the person is given, generally including the following: the place and date of birth, then the place and date of death, followed by any marriage information. This is also the place where biographical information about the person would appear—although the above example lacks any such biographical text.

The birth order for the children, in this case, was indicated with lower-case a, b, c, etc. But the birth order can also be indicated with lower-case roman numerals, such as i, ii, iii, and so on:

1. Franklin WORK
   2. i. Frances Eleanor WORK
      ii. George Paul WORK
   3. iii. Lucy Bond WORK

2. Frances Eleanor WORK

Note that the children without a Register number will not appear again.

Because the numbers continue to rise, and because there are only two columns of numbers to follow, the Register System can be very easy to read, even if the numbers are quite large due to a great number of descendants. For example, say a book was opened in the middle and the numbers appeared as shown below:

3245. James BROWN
    6641. i. William BROWN
    6642. ii. Elizabeth BROWN
    6643. iii. Mary BROWN

3246. Wilma BROWN

This may seem confusing at first, but by understanding the Register System, several rules apply. To find the parents of James Brown, No. 3245, move to the child column and start turning pages toward the front of the book until a child appears with that number. Immediately above that group, the parents will be listed. On the other hand, to find William Brown, No. 6641, as an adult, move to the adult column and start turning pages toward the back of the book. The numbers in both columns are sequential, and all children listed with a number will appear in both columns.

## Problems with the Register Numbering System

There are some fatal flaws built in to the Register System. First, the spouse of the descendant receives no number at all—only the blood line descendants are assigned numbers in the Register System. Moreover, the assignment of Register numbers is dangerous, particularly when further research may reveal the existence of more children of a person. Adding people to the list means that the entire list must be renumbered from that

point. Deleting persons will cause the same sort of problem.

The Register System is the accepted standard for a number of periodicals in America besides *The New England Historical and Genealogical Register*. These periodicals accept manuscripts from genealogists for publication, but the manuscripts must conform to the Register System or the editors will not even read them; therefore, if your goal is to prepare an article for a national magazine, an understanding of the Register System is important.

## The Modified Register System

A variation of the Register System was adapted first by *The New York Genealogical and Biographical Record* and later by the *National Genealogical Society Quarterly*. The New York periodical has since returned to the Register method, but its variation is still called the Record System, while the National Genealogical Society's periodical refers to its method as the Modified Register System.

Here is the same Work family descendancy using the Modified Register System:

1.  Franklin WORK

 + 2.  i. Frances Eleanor WORK
   3.  ii. George Paul WORK
 + 4.  iii. Lucy Bond WORK

2.  Frances Eleanor WORK
   (m. BURKE ROCHE)

   5.  i. Eileen BURKE ROCHE

*(Continued on next page)*

+ 6.  ii.  Cynthia BURKE ROCHE
+ 7.  iii.  Edmund Maurice BURKE ROCHE
  8.  iv.  Francis George BURKE ROCHE

Unlike the Register System, in the Modified Register System every person receives a Register number, an arabic number indicating the line of descent. Every person also receives a lower-case roman numeral indicating the birth order. But unique to the Modified Register System is a symbol that indicates if a child is to be repeated as an adult. The "+" (plus sign) is normally used for this purpose. Even though a child may have a Register number, if no (+) sign appears, that will be the last time that particular name will be seen in the descendancy. To some genealogists, the Modified Register System is considered superior to the Register System because every descendant receives a number.

However, in both systems only the blood-line descendants of number 1 receive a Register number. Spouses of descendants are not part of the descendancy and receive no number at all. The Modified Register System, or Record System, is used by several publications. The genealogist can review these numbering systems in greater detail by visiting a good-sized genealogical library with a sizable family history section. Many published books have a numbering system similar or identical to the Register or Modified Register Systems described above. Variations of these numbering systems exist as well, but again, if the goal is to publish a genealogical article for a national magazine, these two numbering systems should be followed as closely as possible.

# The Henry System

Another system for numbering descendants is called the Henry System. Named after Reginald Henry, the author of a book about the American presidents first published in the 1920s, this system differs radically from either the Register or Modified Register Systems. Using the same descendancy as before, the Henry System appears as shown below:

1 Franklin WORK

    11  Frances Eleanor WORK
    12  George Paul WORK
    13  Lucy Bond WORK

11 Frances Eleanor WORK
   (m. BURKE ROCHE)

    111  Eileen BURKE ROCHE
    112  Cynthia BURKE ROCHE
    113  Edmund Maurice BURKE ROCHE
    114  Francis George BURKE ROCHE

In this system the number identifies the blood-line descendant, as well as the *lineage* back to number 1. Each number is a discrete identification number, an indication of the birth order and the number of generations removed from the person who starts the descendancy.

Franklin Work, as number 1, starts the descendancy. His first child was Frances Eleanor Work. Her number repeats Franklin's number, and then gives her birth order, expressed as a 1; thus, her number is 11. The 4th child of Frances Eleanor Work was Francis George, whose number repeats his mother's number (11), then adds a number indicating his birth order (114) . . . and so on.

The previous example has repeated the two-column arrangement, but this is not a required feature of the Henry System. For example, the descendancy could be tabulated in chart form similar to the example shown in Section 1.

The Henry System numbers can be added to the descendancy diagram as shown below:

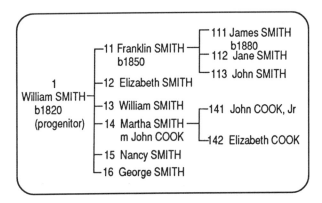

To extend the descendancy using descendant number 142, Elizabeth Cook, her children would be 1421, 1422, 1423, and so on. The descent comes down on either males or females, but is based on the blood-line descendants only. Therefore, as was true in the Register or Modified Register systems, the spouses who marry into the descendancy do not receive a number assignment in the Henry System.

With the Henry System an ID number such as the following is possible for a person:

### 1559856

To read this number, start from right to left: the 6th child, of the 5th child, of the 8th child, of the 9th child, of the 5th child, of the 5th child, of number 1. The descent from number 1 to the person above is as follows:

```
1
  15
    155
      1559
        15598
          155985
            1559856
```

Therefore, to trace the lineage back to the progenitor, just remove the last digit to find the number of the person's blood-line parent. One digit is one generation.

However, there is a problem with the Henry numbers if there are more than 9 children in a family. This is because each digit is meant to represent one generation, so if there is a "13" for a thirteenth child, the double digits would cause the numbers to go awry. So, there are some methods a genealogist can use to indicate a person who was in a family with more than 9 children. In the example above, say that the 9th child should have been the 13th child:

Method 1: 1-5-5-13-8-5-6 (generations separated)
Method 2: 155(13)8565 (double digits only separated)
Method 3: 155-13-856 ("        "    "            ")
Method 4: 155D856 (Hexadecimal)

Any of the above will solve the problem of double digits, but the one that is probably the most useful is Method 4, particularly if a genealogist plans on entering such numbers into a computer. The "D" in Method 4 represents the 13th child.

Hexadecimal numbers have a base of 16 rather than 10 as in decimal numbers. For genealogical use, this would restrict the number of children to 16, but that may not be enough. A comparison of decimal numbers with extended hexadecimal numbers is as follows:

| Decimal | Hexadecimal |
|---------|-------------|
| 1 | 1 |
| 2 | 2 |
| 3 | 3 |
| 4 | 4 |
| 5 | 5 |
| 6 | 6 |
| 7 | 7 |
| 8 | 8 |
| 9 | 9 |
| 10 | A |
| 11 | B |
| 12 | C |
| 13 | D |
| 15 | E |
| 16 | F |
| 17 | G |
| 18 | H |
| 19 | I |
| 20 | J |

. . . and so on . . .

Hexadecimal is base 16, but this will add single-digit numbers for very large families.

Hexadecimal numbers solve the problem of double digit numbers as part of the Henry numbering system because every generation is back to one digit again.

The Register, Modified Register, and Henry Systems all relate to a descendancy. It is assumed that the numbers will be used completely separate from a pedigree project. But there is a way of using the Henry System and combining it with the ahnentafel numbering system. In other words, it is possible to trace ancestors and collateral descendants together in an integrated numbering system.

## Through the Brick Wall

Every genealogist will eventually hit a "brick wall" on a particular lineage.

This occurs when information about a person's parents is seemingly impossible to locate. There is only one way of dealing with a brick wall, and that is to go around it. That is, one must use the *collateral* lines to solve the problem.

For example, a female ancestor who died in childbirth at the age of 16 may have left very few marks to follow. Or, a young man killed in battle may have had a wife and child but never owned land, never left any documents to find in local records, and never appeared in any history books. These are "brick wall" types. But each of these ancestors may have had brothers and sisters who lived to a ripe old age, left many descendants who had documents, family Bibles, memories, etc., and these people are the ones the genealogist must trace to solve the brick wall problems.

Identifying the collateral lines that connect with a pedigree—and then tracing the descendants of those collateral lines—can become unmanageable unless there is a numbering system that integrates both the ahnentafel numbers with a descendancy numbering system. One could think of the pedigree as moving "up" and the descendancy moving "down." The brick wall in the pedigree causes us to move sideways (to a sibling), then down again.

## Combining the Ahnentafel Numbering System with the Henry System

In Section 4, the use of ahnentafel numbers for a pedigree was described. One suggested application of ahnentafel numbers is to identify families. For example, the pedigree diagram could produce ancestors with the following numbers:

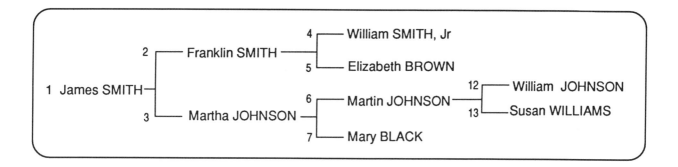

A family sheet can be prepared showing ancestors 12 and 13 as the father and mother. Their pedigree child is ancestor number 6, Martin Johnson. If Martin Johnson had brothers and sisters, they should appear on the sheet as well:

Family No. 12/13

12 William Johnson (father)
13 Susan Williams (mother)

Children:

6.1 William Johnson, Jr.
6.2 Elizabeth Johnson
6 Martin Johnson (ancestor No. 6)
6.4 Mary Johnson, m. James Brown

The technique used to identify the brothers and sisters of Martin Johnson is to add a decimal, then indicate the order of birth. Of course, since Martin Johnson is a full pedigree ancestor (number 6), he cannot have a decimal indicating his birth order, and the 3rd child's position is filled by the pedigree ancestor in this example. (Martin could have been in any birth position and the same full number 6 would be used for him.)

What if a family sheet was needed to show the family of Mary Johnson who married James Brown? There is a method of assigning a sheet number for a collateral sibling—basing the number on the sibling who is the pedigree child, in this case ancestor number 6. This number will be carried on to the next generation to indicate how this collateral line connects with the pedigree.

Family No. 6.4

6.4s James Brown (father)
6.4 Mary Johnson (mother)

Children:

6.41 James Brown, Jr.
6.42 William Brown
6.43 Elizabeth Brown
6.44 Robert Brown
m Angela FRANKLIN

In the above example, a collateral sibling of ancestor number 6 married and had children. This family is not part of the pedigree, but the descendants of the collateral sibling can be identified by linking them to the Ahnentafel Numbering System of the pedigree.

First, a number was created for the spouse of 6.4, and adding a lower-case "s" accomplished that. Then the children of 6.4s and 6.4 were assigned numbers using the *Henry System* for descendants. The key to this combined numbering system is the decimal that separates the two. The decimal acts as a flag and indicates that the person is *not* a pedigree ancestor, but collateral to the pedigree. The ahnentafel number on the left of the decimal indicates how that person connects to the pedigree. The number to the right of the decimal indicates the order of descent, using the Henry System.

Continuing the descent, a family sheet can be prepared for Robert Brown who married Angela Franklin:

---

Family No. 6.44

   6.44    Robert Brown    (Father)
   6.44s  Angela Franklin (mother)

Children:

   6.441  Robert Brown, Jr.
   6.442  William Brown
   6.443  James Brown

---

Any number of collateral families can be identified with this system, all based on the linkage to the pedigree. There is no limit to the steps away from the pedigree, because the Henry System allows an infinite number of descendants. In addition, other non-collateral persons can be incorporated into this system by using the base number to show other relationships. For example, the parents of a spouse can be identified with another signal:

  6.44    Robert Brown (his parents: 6.4 and 6.4s)

  6.44s  Angela Franklin (her parents: 6.44s:2 and 6.44s:4

In the latter example, Angela Franklin married into the descendancy. To give her parents a number, some signal needs to be added indicating that the Henry System has ended and another ahnentafel is beginning. The colon (:) is the signal, and everything to the left of the colon is the same as number 1 on another ahnentafel chart, while to the right of the colon are the ancestors of that person.

If there were multiple marriages for a collateral person, this can be handled too. Adding the lower-case "s" indicates a spouse, but if there were two spouses, they could be shown as:

  6.44s1   (1st spouse)
  6.44s2   (2nd spouse)

Children from a previous marriage of a spouse can be identified by using the number of the spouse, adding another decimal and listing the children:

---

6.44s2      (the 2nd spouse of 6.44)
6.44 s2.s1  (earlier spouse of 6.44s2)

6.44s2.1   (children of 6.44s2
6.44s2.2   from an earlier
6.44s2.3   marriage)

---

There are a variety of techniques to add persons to the numbering scheme, and the above examples give an indication of just some of the methods that can be used. The important part of the Ahnentafel/Henry Numbering System is the number to the left of the decimal, which is the link to the ahnentafel ancestors.

With such a numbering scheme, a genealogist can prepare family sheets for pedigree or collateral families in an integrated system. For example, a list of these sheets in numerical order may appear as shown in the chart below.

In this chart, the numbers having an ahnentafel "2" left of the decimal are arranged before the first family with a "3." This allows many collateral families to be inserted in their own numerical position.

The entire collection of pedigree or collateral families can be filed in one or more notebooks in numerical order using this system, and any descendancy off of the pedigree can be inserted at the appropriate point. There is no requirement that every family be identified, just those families that have a sheet prepared need to be assigned a number. If it is learned later that another family sheet for a collateral line needs to be prepared, the sheet can be integrated with a unique number that does not have any effect on the previous sheets.

```
┌─Pedigree family
│ ┌─Collateral family
│ │ ┌─Family sheet number
```

| | | | |
|---|---|---|---|
| P | | 2/3 | Family of 2, Albert Dollarhide and 3, Marjory (Wiles) Dollarhide |
| | C | 2.1 | Family of Leonard Dollarhide (brother of 2) |
| | C | 2.2 | Family of Dewie (Dollarhide) Fernleaf and husband (daughter of 2.1) |
| | C | 2.11 | Family of Wilma (Dollarhide) Torchie and husband (daughter of 2.1) |
| | C | 3.2 | Family of Francis (Wiles) Lemon (sister of 3) |
| | C | 3.3 | Family of Marybelle (Wiles) Schwald (sister of 3) |
| P | | 4/5 | Family of 4, John C. Dollarhide and 5, Addie (McNemar) Dollarhide |

## Summary

There are three standard numbering systems for a descendancy: (1) the Register System, (2) the Modified Register System, and (3) the Henry System. The first two are the standard methods of preparing an article for the leading genealogical periodicals. The Henry System has many advantages not found in the first two systems and can be combined with the Ahnentafel Numbering System for a pedigree and collateral numbering scheme. This latter system allows a genealogist to file family sheets in numerical order. More importantly, a genealogist can manage a very large number of persons in a logical manner for collateral lines as well as pedigree ancestors.

❂    ❂    ❂    ❂    ❂

# Section 6
# Using a Computer

## Introduction

Today, people entering the field of genealogy for the first time will be inclined to use a computer. This is because the younger people entering the field may have already learned the advantages of the personal computer as an organizational and retrieval tool, and they have fewer biases or fears of the computer. However, most software packages for genealogists seem to be aimed at the family group sheet as the primary recording device. If the computer is to be used primarily as a family sheet printer, the computer may be a gigantic waste of money for the genealogist; in fact, a copying machine might be a better investment.

Before a computer can be used as a truly effective tool, genealogists need to think first in terms of events, not families. They should think in terms of notes and documents, not pedigree charts. They need to utilize the computer as a finding machine, not as a Xerox machine that simply copies pages of information. There are many useful tasks that can be performed with genealogical software; but there are more tasks that can be accomplished with off-the-shelf software, such as a good database manager or word processor.

The most useful task accomplished by a computer is to sort and correlate data, exactly what genealogists do *before* they fill in family group sheets. As I stated above, most genealogical software is aimed at entering information already in the form of a family sheet. The computer, unfortunately, has been reduced to a "copying machine," spitting out nice clean printed reports for you. What about all of the analysis that must take place before a family sheet is prepared? The final reports are important, but perhaps more critical is the work that takes place before the reports are created.

## Computer vs Manual

Any good word processor program can be used to type in text, verbatim documents, extracts, etc., for the myriad of research notes and documents collected in a genealogical project. But how is this an advantage over having the same information typed on a typewriter? Answer: most processor programs have revolutionized typing because editing of text is easier to manage.

Any good database management program allows you to type in columns (fields) of data and then sort these columns in a certain order—all surnames in alphabetical order, for example. How is this an improvement over the manual method? Answer: it saves time, because sorting items manually in alphabetical order can be very time-consuming. But some software packages for genealogy do not offer a database other than the basic vital statistics. (The irony of this is that the database capability is for "after the fact" retrieval, not "before the fact" sorting and analysis.)

## Creating a Database

Section 2 described a manual system for collecting reference material for a genealogical project. The four rules were as follows:

1. Control the sheet size
2. Separate sheets by surname
3. Separate surnames by place of origin
4. Give every sheet a page number

The collection system featured standard 8½" x 11" paper for everything collected, then notebooks for the surnames of interest to the project. The advantage to such a collection is that it does not have to be limited to pedigree ancestors or relatives. The notebooks would contain the known facts found in research, including information about people for whom there is no further information. Information can be collected for people who will never show up on a family sheet—but the information is not lost because it is kept within the same surname book, and then within the section where that person lived.

The disadvantage to such a collection, of course, is that as the collection grows, the genealogist must rely on his or her memory of where to find certain facts. So, an index to the collection becomes important. This can be done using 3" x 5" cards or by making an alphabetical list, citing the page numbers where certain people are located in the collection. Even the simple task of writing a name and a page number can become a mammoth undertaking when the names begin to add up in the thousands. Nonetheless, some method of finding people in the collection will become essential. Rather than just preparing a simple index to the name and page, a genealogist may want to make the index oriented to "events" such as births, deaths, marriages, etc. Here is a suggested list of "data fields" for an index:

1. Given names
2. Surname
3. Type of event
4. Date of event
5. Place of event
6. Type of record
7. Remarks
8. Source code

Imagine a Rolodex or 3" x 5" card index to your reference collection for every name, every event, every place, and every date. With such a card file, the beginnings of a database can be transferred to a computer version easily and logically. An example of one indexed event in the Rolodex file:

```
JOHNSON, John, m1894,
Des Moines, IA, Bible Records
(m Nancy SMITH)

Source: IA 241
```

The key to compiling a good card index is to define the basics, that is, one person, one event, one date, etc. Therefore, in the example above, there needs to be another card for Nancy Smith.

The card index in manual form is the next best thing to a computer, but the computer can turn a Rolodex file into something more sophisticated. Let's say a genealogist creates a computer database file using a standard database management program with the same "fields" as the Rolodex file in the manual system. The hard-copy files have not changed; just the index will be computerized. But now the searching takes on a whole new dimension. For example, the Rolodex file has only one "sort," that is, one specific order, usually in alphabetical order by the last name. But in the computer version, any field can be sorted electronically. This expands the search possibilities dramatically, and you can begin to see why the computer can be used as a finding machine. The Rolodex entry will have to be formalized for the computer, however, and this is where data fields fit in.

An example of a computer database file for the events is shown below:

Such a database file can be very useful because it is not a "linked" file; that is, at this level it is not so important to link every person to a father or mother. It is primarily a "finding" file, where any person can be located in the hard-copy files in more detail. However, a link can be established simply by giving every person an ID number. The index line gives the basic event, name, place, etc.; and the source code indicates where the full record can be found in the documents file. This database file can be sorted in any order: by name, by year, by place, by type of record, or by the source code. Arranging the file so that all Ohio births are on the screen together can be very useful. Or, sorting the file by surname and then printing the file would give a complete index to the surnames mentioned in the entire hard-copy collection.

Therefore, the first step a genealogist can take to computerize records might be something as simple as creating an index. Thinking in terms of computer use can help in organizing a collection for such computer use sometime in the future. When a genealogist is ready to buy a computer and create the electronic index, the logic of the system is already understood; the computer is no longer

| Reference (Index) File | | | | | | | |
|---|---|---|---|---|---|---|---|
| Source Code | ID No. | Soundex Code | Surname, Given | Event Year | State | Locale | Type of Record |
| CA14 | 24 | A145 | AFLINE, Charles | m 1897 | CA | ? | 1900 Census |
| MD20 | 512 | A240 | ASHLEY, John | d 1739 | MD | Kent Co | Will |
| CA57 | 33 | A352 | ADDINGTON, Emma | r 1885 | CA | Cedarville | Death Recd |
| CA57 | 66 | A352 | ADDINGTON, Joe | r 1885 | CA | Cedarville | Death Recd |
| CA25 | 0 | A352 | ADDINGTON, Louise | m 1920 | CA | ? | Fam. History |
| CA25 | 29 | A416 | ALFORD, Meda | m 1880 | CA | Shasta Co | Fam. History |
| CA31 | 112 | A536 | ANDERS, Mrs. Mattie | r 1937 | CA | Shasta Co | Obituary |
| MD06 | 82 | A652 | ARMSTRONG, Thomas | m 1752 | MD | Baltimore | Marriage recd |
| CA11 | 13 | A654 | ARNOLD, Carrie | b 1871 | CA | Merced Co | Cemetery |

just a box with blinking disk lights—it can become an immediate useful tool. And, it can be done using inexpensive database management programs which are readily available at most computer/ software outlets.

## Creating Document Files

On page 43, the use of a word processor on the computer was mentioned. While a database system is designed for structured fields or columns of information for the ease of sorting or searching, a word processor allows text to be entered in a freestyle mode of typing. But added to the text are various features of the software that allow for such things as "global search" routines. Nearly every word processor will have this feature, which can be used to excellent advantage for genealogical text. A global search is used to ask the computer to find a specific phrase or word anywhere in the file. Word processor programs also have the capability of checking spelling, moving text, copying text, etc. This gives a typist a set of tools no typewriter can match.

The well-organized documentation file discussed in Section 2 can also be entered into the computer, either as verbatim text or as abstracted text. In other words, you can use the word processor to copy all of your files and save them on data disks. Organizing the manual files is essential to preparing the same files for the computer. Over a period of time, a genealogist can enter the verbatim text for each document from the hard-copy files. But since this task may be long and tedious, the genealogical project need not collapse while the computer work is underway. Once all of the documentation is on the computer, the genealogist can prepare reports, list index items, compare notes, and do all of the things he would do manually, but with more speed and with confidence that the facts are all together.

## Using a Template File

One suggestion for making the transition to a word processor less difficult is to make use of template files. A template file is a generic file which can be used to type the notes and documents into a consistent format. For example, the RFDS sheet shown on page 10 can be converted into a word processor template file as shown below:

| REFERENCE<br>Family Data Sheet | SURNAME: @<br>Date: @ | Researcher: @ | RFDS NO: @ |
|---|---|---|---|
| Source<br>of<br>Data | @<br>@<br>@ | | |

@

Most word processors have a special search command to find a character, word, or phrase. The *find* criterion is set up by the user first, then a command to find the desired symbol or word is implemented. The cursor will then move to the first occurrence of the desired phrase. Another *find* command will locate the next occurrence, and so on.

In the RFDS template file above, the criterion for the *find* is the @ sign. By finding the first @ sign, the cursor will move to the first position in the template form where something is to be typed. In that field, typing over the @ sign will remove it, and a typist can move quickly from one field to the next field this way. It's like using tab settings on a typewriter.

The typist creates the template form first, saving it as a regular word processor file. The file will be given a name and recalled to the screen easily by calling for the file with that name. Once on the screen, the file name can be changed to something else. (Saving the newly named file will have the effect of leaving the original file unchanged.) Meanwhile, the new file with the new name can be modified by adding data to it.

Another way of accomplishing the same thing is to create the template file, then make a block copy of that file for another use. These features are common among word processor programs, but of course, each works a little differently. In any case a template file copy could be brought to the screen, then new information added, such as in the example below:

| | | |
|---|---|---|
| **REFERENCE** | **SURNAME: DOLLARHIDE** | **RFDS NO: CA70** |
| **Family Data Sheet** | **Date: 3/76** | **Researcher: Wm. Dollarhide** |

| Source of Data | CALIFORNIA DEATH RECORDS, Copied from originals, State Library of California by Dennis Freeman, Sacramento State file No. 17-4833 |
|---|---|

NAME:  Galen Marion DOLLARHIDE    DATE OF DEATH:  31 Jan 1917
PLACE OF DEATH:  Chico, Butte Co CA    DATE OF BIRTH:  22 Feb 1845    PLACE OF BIRTH:  MO
LENGTH AT PLACE OF DEATH:  2 mos.    IN CALIFORNIA:  42 years
SEX:  Male    RACE:  White    MARITAL STATUS:  Married
DIED AT AGE:  71 years, 11 months, 9 days    OCCUPATION:  Farmer
FATHER:  Thomas Dollarhide, born Kentucky    MOTHER:  Elizabeth Cowan, born Kentucky
INFORMANT:  Galen Dollarhide, Fresno, CA    DATE BURIED:  2 Feb 1917
UNDERTAKER: M.E. Engle, Chico, CA

The example above started out as a template file. The file name was changed, and then the document was created. In this case several death certificates were needed, so a new template file was made showing all of the fields for name, place of death, etc. As a result, these items only had to be typed once. It was then possible to create several death records following the exact same format, but in much less time than it would take to type each from scratch.

The form of the template may be identical for all documents, giving some consistency to the typed files in the word processor, and is similar to what is in the hard-copy files. Several template files can be created. For example, birth, death, and marriage certificates, census records, etc., can each have a different blank template file created. As information is typed into the files, redundant typing can be kept to a minimum.

# Ahnentafel/ Henry System Numbers in the Computer

The combined Ahnentafel/Henry System suggested in Section 5 lends itself to computer use quite nicely. A database file can be set up with fields to sort individual records in numerical order, or by date or place of event. For example, a simple database file could be created just for the purpose of sorting people in the pedigree, along with the collateral individuals. The fields need not be lengthy, but a place for the ID number, name, etc., would make it possible to sort by each of these fields.

The first problem encountered in using a computer database is that unless a special routine is programmed, the combined Ahnentafel/Henry numbers cannot be sorted in correct numerical order. This is because text characters for computers have a value based on the American Standard Code for Information Interchange (ASCII). A predetermined order exists for all keyboard characters based on the ASCII numerical value. This causes some of the numbering in the manual system described in Section 5 to

be changed just for computer use. Fortunately, in making these computer-required modifications, the Ahnentafel/ Henry System still works very well. The changes are listed below:

1. Use a modified hexadecimal system to keep all generations as one digit. (A=10, B=11, C=12, etc.)

2. Eliminate the lower-case "s" for a spouse—instead use an asterisk (*).

3. Add a decimal and zero for pedigree ancestors, e.g., a 4 becomes 4.0, 32 becomes 32.0, to give this person the same number of characters (for sorting) as a sibling.

| ID Numbers in a Database | |
|---|---|
| 21.0 | |
| 21.1 | NOTE: Another |
| 21.1* | character that |
| 21.11 | works instead of |
| 21.12 | the asterisk is |
| 21.13 | the dollar sign. |
| 21.13*1 | |
| 21.13*2 | Examples: |
| 21.131 | |
| 21.132 | 21.1$ |
| 22.0 | 21.13$1 |

4. Align numbers on the decimal point. For example, all numbers entered into the database file should have a field for sorting. The field should probably be at least 15 characters across. The numbers entered should all align on the decimal as shown on the next page— since the ASCII value of the asterisk character is less than the value of any alpha or numerical character, the asterisk will sort before a number. This explains why 21.13*1 and 21.13*2 appear before 21.131 and 21.132. Also, note that the pedigree ancestors (21.0 and 22.0) will not sort in their birth

order with siblings. With these modifications in mind, however, a good sort of pedigree and collateral persons can be accomplished, and a database can be created. A proposed layout for a reference file index is shown below:

| REFERENCE FILE INDEX | | | | |
| --- | --- | --- | --- | --- |
| ID NUMBER | A C | SURNAME, GIVEN | BIRTH YEAR/ST | DEATH YEAR/ST |
| 1.0 | A | DOLLARHIDE, William | 1942 WA | — |
| 2.0 | A | DOLLARHIDE, Albert | 1905 OR | 1977 WA |
| 2.1 | C | DOLLARHIDE, Leonard | 1893 CA | 1967 WA |
| 2.1* | C | BUNDY, Belle | 1895 CA | 1979 WA |
| 2.11 | C | DOLLARHIDE, Leo | 1911 WA | — |

The fields above are brief, intended for sorting purposes, and do not give full details. A description of each field follows:

1. ID NUMBER

   This is the place for assigning a person an ID number in the Ahnentafel/ Henry System. Arrangements on this field will sort everyone in numerical order. The only exception is when a person had more than one spouse and had children with each one. In that situation, both spouses' numbers would be listed before those of any of the children.

2. A = ANCESTOR
   C = COLLATERAL

   With these two categories, a sort would be possible for all ancestors first, followed by collaterals.

3. SURNAME, GIVEN

   Combining these names into a single field takes care of several persons with the same surname, then alphabetizes them by given name. If a sort by first name only is desired, then two fields should be created.

4. BIRTH YEAR/ST

   Birth year and state of birth. A full description is probably not necessary.

5. DEATH YEAR/ST

   Death year and state of death.

This suggested database file in the computer is something that can be created quite easily. With all persons entered into a file, it is possible to sort the file by surname and to print an index. The file can then be sorted again and a list printed by birth or death year; or it can be sorted for all ancestors, or all collaterals. The file order can be returned to the Ahnentafel/Henry order by sorting that field again.

A computer genealogist can design a format similar to the database shown above, or create his own sorting files. The use of the Ahnentafel/Henry System allows for some creative sorting, regardless of the other fields in the database.

# Genealogical Computing Resources

At this point we should note that there are some important genealogical services and products available to computer users. In addition to commercial genealogical software, there are magazines, online services, and genealogical databases. Highlights of the most significant resources are given below. This information is provided along with addresses to which you can write for more details. First, the principal categories:

- **Genealogical Computing Periodicals.** Only a few reliable sources provide state-of-the-art information about what is happening in this highly specialized field. Two of the best computing periodicals are described.

- **Information Retrieval.** This category includes LDS Family History Library databases, CD-ROM databases from private vendors, and genealogical sources on the Internet, all of which are described in more detail.

- **GEDCOM Utility.** This method of exchanging genealogical information has become a standard. The LDS Family History Library uses this utility for downloading files from their main-frame computer databases to personal computers. In addition, several genealogical software developers use GEDCOM for importing or exporting files to or from different systems. A brief description of GEDCOM is included.

- **Commercial Genealogical Software.** A brief review of the most popular software packages is given, along with addresses for requesting more information.

# Periodicals

## Genealogical Computing

Published since 1980, this quarterly journal has become the leader in providing reviews, articles, and general information about using computers in genealogy. The quality continues to improve and the magazine is well presented and timely. Annual features include guides to software, databases, and utilities for genealogical computer applications. *Genealogical Computing* employs contributing editors who are extremely knowledgeable and provide excellent articles about software or new ideas in using computers for genealogy. A subscription is currently $25.00 per year for four issues. For more information write to the publisher, Ancestry.com, Inc., 266 W. Center St., Orem, UT 84057. Toll-free phone: 1-800-531-1790. Internet: **http://www. ancestry.com/gencomp/index.htm**

## NGS/CIG Digest

Since 1981 the Computer Interest Group (CIG) of the National Genealogical Society (NGS) has published a quarterly newsletter. The *NGS/CIG Digest* continues to provide valuable up-to-date information on genealogical software, utilities, Internet services, and the general state of the field. To receive this newsletter you must be a member of the National Genealogical Society. For $40.00 per year, NGS members receive the *National Genealogical Society Quarterly* plus the *NGS Newsletter*, which gives timely information about what is happening nationally in genealogical circles.

In addition, NGS members who specify an interest in the *NGS/CIG Digest* receive this newsletter without any extra charge. To obtain an application for NGS membership write to the National Genealogical Society, 4527 17th St. N., Arlington, VA 22207-2399. The membership application form has a place where you can indicate your interest in receiving the *NGS/CIG Digest*. You can also visit the NGS web site: **http://www. ngsgenealogy.org**

# Information Retrieval

Perhaps the most exciting development in genealogical computing has been the advent of computer databases which can now be accessed by the public, making a preliminary search for ancestors easier and quicker. For example, the Family History Library of The Church of Jesus Christ of Latter-day Saints (LDS) has for many years been developing major main-frame computer databases for genealogical research. These databases are now available outside of Salt Lake City. In addition, a few private companies have begun services to provide large database information for genealogists, including indexes to vital records for parts of the U.S. Online services, such as America Online (AOL), have "round-tables" where persons using a computer and a modem can use their home telephone to access and exchange genealogical information, leave messages, and share with other genealogists. In addition, the World Wide Web of the Internet has become a tremendous source for learning about genealogical information. The best of these information sources are listed in more detail below:

## Family History Library Databases

The LDS Family History Library in Salt Lake City has several major com-puter database files, all accessed through a system referred to as FamilySearch™, which contains (1) a catalog of the entire holdings of the library—the largest genealogical library in the world; (2) the International Genealogical Index™ (IGI), which is an index of names, dates, and places with over 300 million entries; (3) the Ancestral File™, a linked database with several million entries and growing rapidly; and (4), the Social Security Death Index, which contains an index to deaths in the U.S. since 1962 (and some as far back as the 1930s). The FamilySearch databases have been published on CD-ROM disks and are found at thousands of LDS Family History Centers in the U.S. and Canada. At one of these locations, a computer genealogist can print copies from these files or download information to a diskette that can be used on a personal computer. It is very easy to locate the nearest Family History Center—just check a local phone book for an LDS church and call for information about its nearest library and hours of operation, or write to Family History Library, 50 East North Temple St., Salt Lake City, UT 84150, or call (801) 240-2399. The FamilySearch databases are also available on the Internet: **http:// www. familysearch.com**

## CD-ROM Databases

Besides the Family History Library, there are several companies that produce CD-ROM databases for genealogists. The largest publisher is Brøderbund. Brøderbund is the publisher of the Family Tree Maker™ (FTM) software. Through FTM or a separate search program, a genealogist can search his CD-ROM drive and use hundreds of different databases. Included are millions of indexed marriage records showing brides, grooms, dates, places, etc., for several states, plus name indexes to census records, 1790–1860; indexes to immigrants arriving in the U.S.; indexes to statewide vital records, and many more databases.

Similar to the Family Tree Maker series, the Ultimate Family Data Library by Palladium Interactive offers a number of CD-ROM databases, as does the Generations Grande Suite by Sierra Home. See a review of these systems under "Genealogical Software" below.

A company that produces stand-alone CD-ROM databases is Heritage Quest (HQ) of Bountiful, Utah. The HQ databases include marriages, vital records, and the best indexes to the 1870 census for all states. HQ has scanned the microfilmed images for all manuscript census records 1790–1920, and these are now available on CDs as well.

## The GEDCOM Utility

GEDCOM stands for Genealogical Data Communications and is a standard method of organizing files with linked genealogical information. The standard is the format in which a file is saved by the computer so other software with the GEDCOM utility can use the same data. Created by the LDS Library computer staff for their own needs, it has become available to all genealogical software developers who agree to the standards. Each software developer must design a GEDCOM utility that works with its own software. GEDCOM does nothing by itself, and it should be used in addition to a genealogical software system.

To explain what GEDCOM does, imagine a Frenchman who speaks no German trying to speak to a German who speaks no French. When the two discover that they both speak English, they can communicate. GEDCOM is a "second language" understood by several different software systems so they can transfer files to one another. As long as two software systems have a GEDCOM utility, communicating is a matter of "translating" databases and text information into a GEDCOM format they both understand.

The LDS Family History Library uses the GEDCOM utility as a means of creating files from their large main-frame databases such as the IGI and Ancestral File. They also use GEDCOM as a means of inputting into their databases information gathered from many different computer users. Most developers have included a GEDCOM utility in their commercial software packages so these transfers can take place.

The importance of GEDCOM to computer genealogists is that it allows you to use more than one software system by entering names, dates, places, notes, etc., in one system, then creating a GEDCOM file for the purpose of transferring that information to a completely different software system. The result is that you do not have to enter the information from scratch again to take advantage of other software with different features. It should be mentioned, however, that some genealogical software developers interpret the GEDCOM standards differently, and there are some inconsistencies between each of them. Improvements to the GEDCOM standard will continue to be made.

# Genealogical Software

A recent book by Marthe Arends, *Genealogy Software Guide* (Baltimore: Genealogical Publishing Co., 1998), identifies 84 different genealogical software packages from all over the world. The book shows many examples of the software available to genealogists and for most types of computers. It is a valuable guide that can be used in selecting genealogical software.

Brief reviews of the most popular genealogical software systems are given below, based, in part, on reviews from *Heritage Quest* magazine (with the permission of the editor, Leland Meitzler). The five full-service genealogy programs chosen for this review are as follows:

1. *Family Tree Maker* by Brøderbund Software.
2. *Ultimate Family Tree* by Brøderbund Software.
3. *Generations* by Sierra Home.
4. *The Master Genealogist* by Wholly Genes Software.

In addition to the above four programs, a special genealogical document and evidence utility program, *Clooz*, by Ancestor Detective, will be reviewed.

This description of genealogical software will be limited to the above products, not only because they are widely used, but because they all have met some basic criteria which should be used to evaluate genealogical software. For example, they all have support via telephone or the Internet; they all have the GEDCOM utility; they all have many features besides the ability to print charts and forms and are considered comprehensive software systems. In addition, all of the developers have demonstrated a dedication to improve their products with new enhancements and upgrades.

## Family Tree Maker™

This popular genealogical software has come a long way since it was first released in 1989 because the developer has responded to genealogists' requests for more and more features. Data entry into Family Tree Maker is very easy. Just enter the names, dates, locations, and facts on a Family page. Tabs (like you find on file folders) on the side of the page allow you to move between generations. If you want to move to someone else's page, just click on the index button and type the name. Unlimited numbers of events and facts can be entered for each person, and conflicting information can be entered. In addition, you can enter photos, scanned documents, even video clips into the "scrapbook." The visuals can be manipulated within the program and added to printed reports.

The Family Tree Maker deluxe version comes with several CD-ROM disks which include World Family Tree™ listings of millions of names submitted by FTM users from their pedigrees, plus the Social Security Death Index, and other databases.

**System Requirements:** Windows 95/98, CD-ROM drive (2x or higher), 486 or faster processor, 8 MB RAM—16 MB recommended, minimum 20 MB hard drive space, 640x480 display—16 colors or higher.

**Available from:** Brøderbund Software, Parsons Division, 1700 Progress Drive, PO Box 100, Hiawatha, IA 52233-0100. Toll-free phone: (800) 474-8696. Internet: http://www.familytreemaker. com/

### Ultimate Family Tree™

Many reviewers have proclaimed this program to be the very best genealogy program available for the serious genealogist. The program will do just about anything that a researcher might want to do, and it is not terribly difficult to use. The program is an outgrowth of the very popular "Roots" series of software which was known for allowing great latitude in the way a genealogist might want to organize, sort, and present his data.

Ultimate Family Tree allows the user to enter data in a normal way or advanced editing mode. Those new to the program are advised to use the normal editing mode. This seems to be in response to those who have complained that the program was too hard to run. The data entry is very straightforward and is made on the Individual Record screen. The name, sex, whether living, and event type, date, and place are all entered on this screen by clicking on buttons at the bottom of the screen. A GEDCOM file can be imported easily. A typical system can import a 4,500 name file in a little over three minutes, at the same time making a number of conversions in the data. The conversions include changing names that were in "all capitals" to names with only the first letters of the name capitalized.

A good selection of reports and charts—such as fan charts, ancestor and descendancy reports, and so forth—are available. Hundreds of report options are also available. Photos and documents can be stored, manipulated, and printed.

The software is supported on the Internet, where additional services—such as a subscription to the Ultimate Family Data Library, lineage searches, sample subscriptions to magazines, and special offers to purchase other software—are available.

The Ultimate Family Data Library is accessible through this software, although each CD-ROM disk from the Data Library must be purchased separately. The library consists of several databases, including U.S. Ports Passenger Lists, Virginia and Pennsylvania Records, and the 1910 New York City census.

**System Requirements:** Windows 95/98, CD-ROM drive (2x or higher), Pentium processor, 16 MB RAM, minimum 50 MB hard disk space.

**Available from:** Brøderbund Software, Parsons Division, 1700 Progress Drive, PO Box 100, Hiawatha, IA 52233-0100. Toll-free phone: (800) 548-1806. Internet: http://www.ultimatefamilytree. com/

### Generations Grande Suite™

This is a great program. Not only does *Generations* make entering and analyzing data and printing reports easy to do, but included with the program is one of the best collections of names and data to be distributed with any genealogy program. The program and collection comes on 12 CDs. One CD has the program, *MasterCook Heritage Edition*, and a names glossary on it. Another includes *SnapShot*™ photo-enhancing software and historic records. CD 3 has a Civil War roster on it. CDs 4 and 5 have the Social Security Death Index on them, and CDs 6 to 12 are a World Name Index. Included with the program is a copy of Cyndi Howell's best selling *Netting Your Ancestor*s (Baltimore: Genealogical Publishing Co., 1997), not an electronic copy, but the book itself. This alone is a $20.00 value.

Generations is based originally on the popular Reunion for Windows program. The screen is made up such that data for a husband and wife are on the screen next to each other. Above them are the names of their parents and their marriage data. This screen is unique. Just click on the name, and data entry screens come up. Sources are also added from this screen. Like all other good genealogy programs, sources only need to be entered once and can be referred to whenever needed, but this software allows you to click on "show links" to get a list of all individuals to whom a particular source refers. The program allows the user to enter stepchildren and adopted children, linking to more than one set of parents.

Charting is one of the strengths of this program. You can move the graphic boxes and branches around on the screen by just dragging them into place. The "hourglass" chart showing ancestors and descendants is clever and a user can add, delete, and edit boxes on the chart screen and manipulate them in other ways.

Many reports can be created, including an ahnentafel, Register (book style), or descendancy chart, and the program will automatically export any report to a user's word processor. In the word processor a user can modify or customize the report further.

Included with the program are indexes that give the user access to over 200 million names and data. The program also includes a link to *CyndisList* on the Internet (**http://www. CyndisList.com**), a place to locate hundreds of genealogy-related web sites.

**System Requirements:** Windows 95/98, Pentium 100 with SVGA color monitor, 640x480 set at 256 colors (Pentium 166 with 88-x600 and 16-bit high color preferred), 2x CD-ROM (24x preferred), 16 MB of RAM (24 MB preferred), 20 MB of hard disk space, Windows compatible mouse and printer; Optional: 14.4 bps modem (33.6 preferred) and 32-bit Internet Service Provider (ISP).

**Available from:** Havas Interactive, PO Box 629000, El Dorado Hills, CA 95762. Toll-free phone: (800) 757-7707. Internet: www.sierra.com/sierrahome/familytree/

### The Master Genealogist™

In many respects this program is the most comprehensive genealogy software on the market, and the one that many professional genealogists use. It is the software that people upgrade to when they want even more features and capabilities from their genealogical software.

The software handles genealogical events (births, deaths, christenings), and any dated event, such as a residence, can be entered in unlimited quantities, each with sources attached to them. Conflicting evidence can be entered, listed, and analyzed. Pedigrees can be navigated, moving forward or backward, and a person will be shown with all siblings. This system is very efficient and allows for locating any person in any generation quickly, without knowing a name, date, or ID number for a person.

There are three view screens: The Person View is a summary of all the information that has been entered on one person. The Person View screen lists the subject's name and ID number. Below that, most data is found in one of two boxes, the Tag Box or the Flag Box. All the events in a person's life are found in the Tag Box. Dated events are in chronological order. To enter an event, click on the + icon, pick the type of event you might want, hit Enter, and get the Tag Entry screen. On this screen, your data is entered, as are your citations. Once a source citation is entered, it need never be typed again. Just pick it from the master list, or by entering a "source number." You can also mark how sure you are of the reliability of a source.

The Family Screen shows the subject, spouse, parents of both, and children along with children's spouses, with birth and death statistics for each person.

The Tree View shows a five-generation pedigree chart with the subject in the first position. The siblings and children of the subject are listed. By clicking on any one of these names, that person will move into the first position. To add a relative of the person in the first position, just click on the "add a new person" icon at the top of the screen. Pick from a choice of parents, siblings, children, or an unrelated person, and enter that data— a simple task.

The database has unique searching capabilities, using the "pick-list" to search for a name as a string of characters with any part of the program, or searching by the first name of person, place, or any other event or field contents. A user can run a Place Frequency report in which a particular place can be analyzed.

The package includes the entire U.S. Geological (USGS) place-name database of about 2 million named places in the U.S., including hills, valleys, towns, cemeteries, etc. For example, over 107,000 named cemeteries are in this database. A place found in this database will be linked to a map number, so a particular map can be ordered from USGS or found and printed on the USGS Internet web site. This is a tremendous resource for genealogists.

The reports generated by this software are very complete. Multimedia presentations are possible as well. Of all the genealogical software, this one has the most database arrangements, lists, searching reports, or just statistical reports for analysis of a genealogical project.

*The Master Genealogist* has more whistles and bells than the others and may be more of a challenge to a beginning computer person. For that reason, it is usually the software that genealogists upgrade to after they have entered data into another system. In addition to the GEDCOM utility for exporting or importing files, this software includes conversion routines so that the database files of other genealogical software can be converted directly, with no loss of data. The user can pick from a list of databases created by other software systems which *The Master Genealogist* will recognize and import directly. No other genealogical software has this capability. It is not surprising that this software is the choice of professional genealogists.

**System Requirements:** IBM compatible computer (386 required, 486 or higher recommended); Windows 3.x, 95/98, NT or OS/2; 8 MB memory (16 MB recommended); hard drive, mouse, VGA or higher resolution monitor; Optional: Windows compatible printer, Twain-compatible scanner, Soundblaster or compatible sound card.

**Available from:** Wholly Genes Software, 5144 Flowertuft Court, Columbia, MD 21044. Toll-free phone: 1-877-TMG-FAMILY. Internet: http:// www. whollygenes.com

## Clooz™

This utility software is a database manager of genealogical evidence. It can be used to index, sort, and analyze the documentary evidence that we all have in our collections. The database has premade forms for entering data from the 1790 through 1920 U.S. censuses, and from Irish, British, and Canadian censuses; people; city directories; photographs; and miscellaneous documents.

It is recommended that a user sort his or her documents into a logical order—by document type (census, probate, birth, etc), family, surname, or whatever system the researcher might want to use. Genealogists following the concepts of this book in organizing original source material will find Clooz a great way to document their genealogical project, using a surname-place-page number for every document. This method can be adopted into Clooz very well so that all documents are in computer form and relate to the paper documents by a source code.

This is not genealogical software for entering information about individuals—it is software for entering information from the notes and documents collected in a genealogical project and for the people mentioned in a document. Every document can be numbered, and every person mentioned in a document can be assigned a number. With a well-organized manual system, it is possible to continue the numbers used manually into this computer system—a good way to completely convert a paper system to a computer.

All genealogists have large collections of source data, some for known ancestors, collateral ancestors, or from suspicious people. This program allows a genealogist to extract and index these documents.

**System Requirements:** The program is available as a stand-alone program or to be used with Microsoft Access 97. It runs under Windows 95 or 98, or NT3.51 or higher, and requires 30 MB hard disk space (for stand-alone program), and a CD-ROM drive.

**Available from:** Ancestor Detective, PO Box 6386, Drawer B, Plymouth, MI 48170-8486. Phone: 734-354-6449. Internet: http://www.ancestordetective. com/clooz.htm

# Section 7

# Presentation Techniques

## Introduction

One of the biggest challenges facing a genealogist is in communicating the results of his research to non-genealogists. Many researchers with years of experience have still not published the results of their work, mainly because a genealogical project can never be totally finished. But if there were some techniques to make that job easier, perhaps more limited genealogical reports could be distributed, making the current research available to other researchers.

This section will suggest some methods for getting the results prepared in a format that can be published, privately or commercially. "Published" in this context can mean a photocopied set of notes and documents, with a brief narrative describing the nature of the project, or a full book published privately or by a commercial book publisher.

In any case, leaving a published account of your years of research and effort is something that should be done, even if the project is not complete. Webster says that "to publish" can mean "to make public." That is exactly what genealogists should do with their work, and the act of making the work public may be nothing more than providing copies to a local library or sending a few copies out to various members of the family.

## Pedigree Presentation—
### Using Pedigree Ancestor Index Sheets

The pedigree charts that many genealogists use regularly as worksheets can provide the basis for a formal presentation of the project. However, printing a stack of pedigree charts might not be too meaningful to a non-genealogist, particularly if the charts are those that have the same numbers on every sheet.

Based on the concepts described earlier, the use of ahnentafel numbers provides an excellent index to all pedigree ancestors—and the Ahnentafel/Henry Numbering System can integrate the collateral people into the project. Therefore, a pedigree chart that is designed just to show the ahnentafel numbers and the names can serve as an index to the pedigree.

An example of such a special pedigree chart is shown on page 60. This

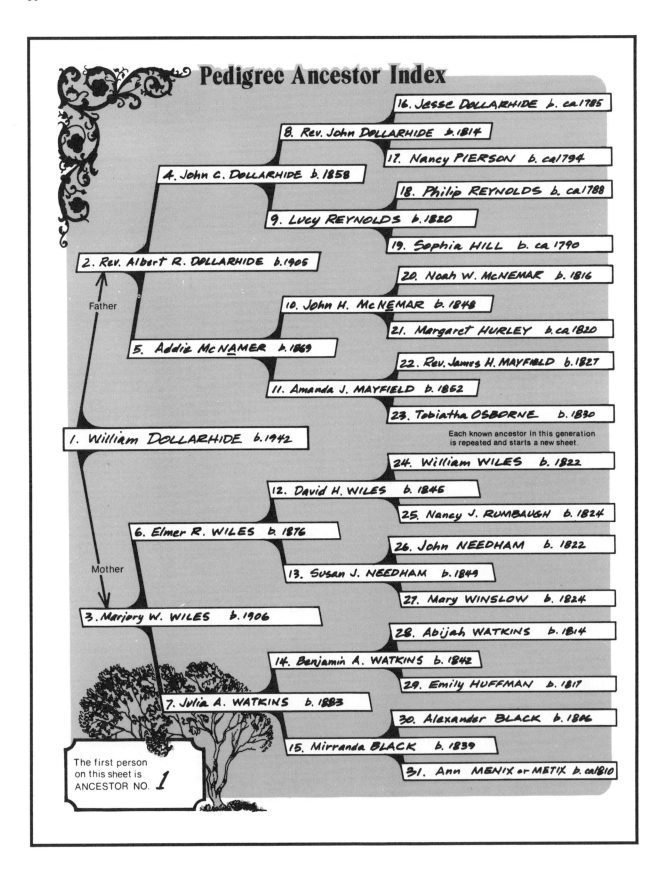

# Pedigree Ancestor Index

16. Jesse DOLLARHIDE  b. ca 1785

8. Rev. John DOLLARHIDE  b. 1814

17. Nancy PIERSON  b. ca 1794

4. John C. DOLLARHIDE  b. 1858

18. Philip REYNOLDS  b. ca 1788

9. Lucy REYNOLDS  b. 1820

19. Sophia HILL  b. ca 1790

2. Rev. Albert R. DOLLARHIDE  b. 1905

20. Noah W. McNEMAR  b. 1816

Father

10. John H. McNEMAR  b. 1848

21. Margaret HURLEY  b. ca 1820

5. Addie McNAMER  b. 1869

22. Rev. James H. MAYFIELD  b. 1827

11. Amanda J. MAYFIELD  b. 1852

23. Tobiatha OSBORNE  b. 1830

Each known ancestor in this generation
is repeated and starts a new sheet.

1. William DOLLARHIDE  b. 1942

24. William WILES  b. 1822

12. David H. WILES  b. 1845

25. Nancy J. RUMBAUGH  b. 1824

6. Elmer R. WILES  b. 1876

26. John NEEDHAM  b. 1822

13. Susan J. NEEDHAM  b. 1849

Mother

27. Mary WINSLOW  b. 1824

3. Marjory W. WILES  b. 1906

28. Abijah WATKINS  b. 1814

14. Benjamin A. WATKINS  b. 1842

29. Emily HUFFMAN  b. 1817

7. Julia A. WATKINS  b. 1883

30. Alexander BLACK  b. 1806

15. Mirranda BLACK  b. 1839

The first person
on this sheet is
ANCESTOR NO. 1

31. Ann MENIX or METIX  b. ca 1810

chart is called a "Pedigree Ancestor Index." It was designed specifically for using ahnentafel numbers, so there are no ID numbers printed on the charts. The ahnentafel numbers need to be entered on the form along with the names. The form was also designed to serve as the first section in a published notebook, to prepare a reader for things to come.

The ahnentafel index could be followed by all of the pertinent Compiled Family Data Sheets (CFDS) (see page 17), again organized in numerical order. Each CFDS continuation sheet provides a place to list all references used for that family, and the references themselves could be incorporated into the notebook.

Such an organization is logical and easy to follow. But, a non-genealogist may still need some help in understanding what the book contains and how it is organized. Here is a sample explanation that could be the first page in the notebook:

"This book is divided into three (3) major sections:

1.  The Pedigree Ancestor Index gives every ancestor an ID number. If a pedigree line continues on to another Pedigree Index Sheet, use the number of the desired ancestor in the last row (generation) to the right; that person will then be repeated as the first person on another chart extending the pedigree.

2.  Family sheets are also organized by the ID numbers, using the ID number of the husband and the wife. For example, to find the family of ancestor 12, there will be a family sheet for 12/

13 showing all of the known children and more information about the family in general.

The continuation sheet for each family lists all references that have been found for that family. Each reference item is organized by surname, place, and sheet number. The place will be coded using the two-letter post office codes, such as MA for Massachusetts, IN for Indiana, and so on.

3.  The reference sheets are found in the third section, and these sheets support the notes and documents from which all of the family sheets were prepared. Each reference sheet has a page number indicating surname, place, and sheet number. They are all organized in alphabetical order by the surname, then the place, and within each place section, by sheet number."

The explanatory page will prepare a reader for what is to come, and the organization of the material will serve its purpose much better.

## Pedigree Presentation—
### Using Master Data Sheets

Another method that provides the reader with an overview of the pedigree presentation is to replace the Pedigree Ancestor Index Sheet form with the Master Data Sheet form (see page 20). The same basic arrangement can be used: that is, start with the Master Data Sheets in numerical order, followed by the Compiled Family Data Sheets, and all the reference sheets. Again, an explanation to the reader is helpful. The paragraph below could replace the first paragraph that was used in the previous example:

"1. The Master Data Sheet (MDS) gives the basic vital statistics and a discrete ID number for every known pedigree ancestor in this notebook. The person who starts the pedigree is the first sheet, followed thereafter in numerical order by each ancestor who has been identified. The ID number is also used to find the families. For example, to find the family of ancestor number 12, the family sheet will be 12/13, organized in numerical order."

# Biographies

A written narrative is usually easier to understand than a group of forms. A pedigree publication identifies many ancestors, along with other people collateral to the pedigree. But to bring the names, places, and dates into perspective, a biographical sketch about each pedigree person would enhance the publication and give life to the presentation.

Several techniques can be utilized; for example, a brief biography for each person might be prepared, and each biography could follow the family sheet where that person's vital statistics are given. Or, a group of biographies could be written one after another in numerical order, using the ahnentafel numbers for each. The length of the biography required depends on the information available. A partial, sample biography is shown as follows:

**"16. Jesse Dollarhide**

Jesse Dollarhide was probably a son of Hezekiah Dollarhide, but not enough evidence exists to prove that linkage. Evidence indicates that Jesse was born about 1785–1790 in Randolph County, North Carolina. He was known to have lived near Hezekiah on an adjoining farm in Harrison Township, Wayne County, Indiana. The 1820 and 1830 censuses indicate that both men lived there for about 10 years. In 1813, in Preble County, Ohio, Jesse married Nancy Pierson, a daughter of Thomas and Nancy Pierson. It was soon after their marriage that land records and other references show Jesse residing in Wayne County, Indiana . . . ."

At the conclusion of the biography, a list of the references that were used to make the statements about the person could be given. The list of references may already be part of the Master Data Sheet or the Compiled Family Data Sheet, but for an overview of the references used in a biographical sketch, another list may be useful. Historical researchers sometimes use this technique as a means of providing a synopsis of the critical source items for certain facts. This is usually done freestyle, and one method is shown below:

**REFERENCES—Jesse Dollarhide (ID16)**

**Birth**: see RFDS NC 34, 35, and 36
**Marriage**: see RFDS OH 14
**Residence in Wayne Co IN**: see RFDS IN 12, 13, 14, 15, 21, 34, 45, 67, 83, and 103
**Residence in Fountain Co IN**: see RFDS IN 16, 17, 18, and 101
**Estate**: see RFDS IN 102, 103, 104, and 107
**Heirs**: see RFDS IN 43, 44, 67, 83, 103, and 107

Note that in the example above, source codes can be used. Even though the reference citation for IN 12 might be "1820 Federal Census, Wayne Co., Indiana . . .," that sheet was given the designation IN 12 in the reference collection. This source code can only be used if the references have been well organized and easy to retrieve—therefore, the importance of the notes and documents comes into play again. Nothing worthwhile can be done without well-organized notes and documents.

## Descendancy Presentation Techniques

In America the standard way to present a descendancy is to use either the Register System or the Modified Register System. Examples of these numbering systems are shown in Section 5, but what is not shown are methods of listing the references used to compile a descendancy.

Citing sources in narrative writing is important, but genealogists sometimes have a special problem due to the nature of the documents used to compile the narrative. For example, genealogists must deal not only with books but also with microfilm, original correspondence, original court documents, oral interviews, personal memories, and many other published narrative sources. Yet any published narrative attempting to be academically acceptable should follow academia's rules. For that reason, source codes should probably not be used in any formal narrative if the Register System is used. Instead, full bibliographic citations

should be given, following the standard form used for reference books.

A book that is invaluable for genealogical narrative writing is Richard S. Lackey's *Cite Your Sources* (New Orleans: Polyanthos, Inc., 1980). In addition, see a more recent book by Elizabeth Shown Mills, *Evidence! Citation and Analysis for the Family Historian* (Baltimore: Genealogical Publishing Co., 1997).

In writing a narrative family history, it is acceptable practice to conclude the narrative with a list of sources, as in a bibliography. However, a genealogical descendancy can be quite large, and it can be irritating to have to refer constantly to the back of the book to check the citations. But if the book can be organized into logical groups of people, or into chapters, it is perfectly acceptable to list the sources following the conclusion of the narrative for the group or at the end of the chapter.

## Other Methods in Presenting a Descendancy

Although most non-genealogists could probably decipher the Register System or Modified Register System, neither is immediately comprehensible without an understanding of the numbers and the way the formatting works. Therefore, for a simple presentation to family members, a chart or diagram may have some great advantages.

During the course of collecting information for a descendancy, it may be necessary to contact many people who share a relationship with you. It is frustrating to write letters to distant cousins who are not particularly interested in genealogy, and getting a response to the letters may not be easy. However, one technique that can increase the odds of getting that response is to present that person with a gift of a chart or diagram, perhaps "obligating" the person to respond. This devious tactic has helped many experienced genealogists. Here is how it works:

1. Prepare a clever diagram that clearly shows the position of the person in the descendancy.

2. Send two copies of the diagram to the person with a personal note requesting him to "correct any errors and return one copy . . . ."

3. Promise to send "full details" at no cost if the person will cooperate by sending more information.

4. Mention that all of the "important" people in the family will be given a special biography, illustrated with photographs.

5. Watch the mailbox for an early response.

This may appear somewhat tongue-in-cheek, but the author has used this technique with excellent results. (This one works almost as well as the newspaper ad in the "Personals" section of the local newspaper which declares, "Salt Lake City attorney seeking legal heirs of Lafayette Black . . . all responses private and personal." It drives them crazy with curiosity!)

Of course, the offer to provide "more information" assumes that a publication is forthcoming. Giving out charts and diagrams of the project before the full details are complete has at least three results:

1. The compiler gains an understanding of what is known and what is not known.

2. The response rate will be higher due to the charts, and the chances of getting more information are therefore higher as well.

3. The chart becomes a working outline for a forthcoming publication.

You don't have to be artistic to compile a good diagram. A typewriter or word processor can be used effectively, or the diagram can be plotted by hand. But if some techniques are understood, the diagram can become a very important tool in developing the full descendancy for the final publication.

## Descendancy Diagram Techniques

One method of diagraming a descendancy is to use columns of names in the same generations, and lines tracing the descent for the families as seen below:

The Register numbers should be added in pencil, because as new information comes to light, the numbers may have to change.

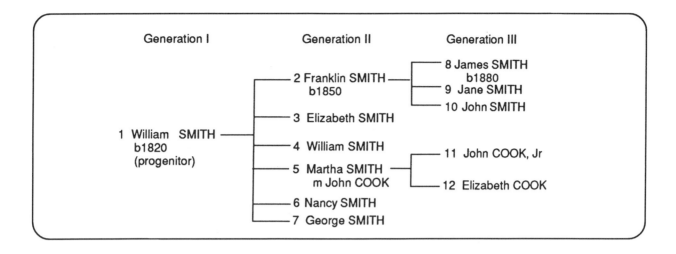

The diagram becomes increasingly complicated in each generation due to the numbers of persons in the same generation. As new information is found, the numbers will change and the arrangement of the chart will change. For example, say that No. 3, Elizabeth Smith, was discovered to have had five descendants. Inserting these into Generation III would cause all later descendants in that generation to slide down. The Register numbers would have to be changed to reflect the inserted descendants, and all descendants listed after the inserted names would need to be renumbered as well. An illustration of these added names is shown in the following diagram:

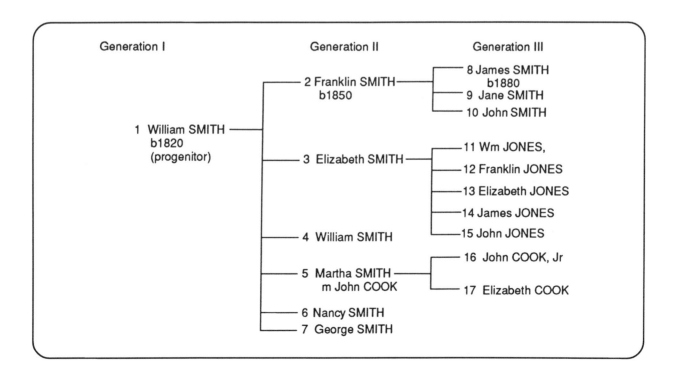

The diagram becomes even more complicated if there are great numbers of people in a single generation, and it would seem impossible to chart them all unless a very large sheet of paper was used. But with the first diagram sketched in pencil, modified as new information is revealed, 8½" x 11" sheets will be sufficient, provided continuation sheets are used. About four generations can be placed on one sheet, and for continuation sheets the same sort of chart continuation as was used on a pedigree chart can be used. The chart number could be the same as the first person on the sheet.

Before a final typewritten version is produced, the individual families can be typed up, as in the example below. This entire family can be cut out with scissors, along with the other families in that generation. The cut-outs can then be arranged loosely on a blank page to enable you to visualize the spacing and create a mock-up for the final typing.

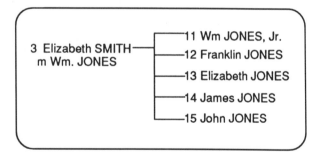

## Showing More Than One Spouse

A method of showing spouses of descendants is to list the spouse directly below the person being diagramed. The spouses who marry into the descendancy are not blood-line descendants of the first progenitor, but they should always be in-

cluded. If a descendant had more than one spouse, it is possible to show all of them, indicating which children derived from which spouse:

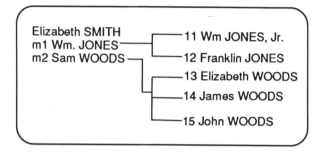

## Using Labels

To add a graphic touch, consider using self-adhesive labels, which can be very effective in showing the same descendancy. Labels are available, usually in sheets, from any good stationery store. A good size for one person on a descendancy is about ½ inch by 2½ inches. Labels will make the whole chart much larger, but they also will make it look better. A typewriter can be used to type names on the labels. Then the labels can be peeled off the backing sheet and arranged on a blank page to construct the descendancy diagram. An example of a family in a descendancy using these labels is shown below:

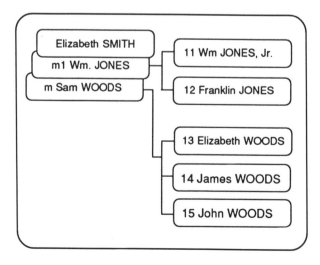

Offsetting the labels for the spouses below a descendant adds a visual effect and makes the chart more interesting. After positioning the labels and sticking them to a blank page, the lines can be drawn. The easiest way to draw the lines is to use a fine-point felt marker. The outline of each label can be traced easily if the pen is placed against the edge of the label, using the edge to guide the pen point around it. A very professional appearance can result, because when the chart is photocopied, the labels will not show except as uniform outlined boxes.

To draw the connecting straight lines, use a straight-edge plastic ruler, such as a see-through school ruler. Draw the lines lightly in pencil first, confirm that everything looks straight, then draw the straight lines using the felt-tip pen. When the ink is completely dry, the pencil lines can be removed with a soft eraser, leaving clean inked lines connecting all the label boxes.

The purpose of preparing a descendancy graphically is to have an outline of the families in a clear, visual form. More importantly, sending such a chart to a relative—perhaps a total stranger—increases the chances of getting a good response and therefore more information. The relative who receives the chart will have an immediate understanding of the descendancy. If that person's name appears on the chart, the chances are good that a response will be forthcoming. A picture is worth a thousand words!

❀    ❀    ❀    ❀    ❀

# Research Journal

William Dollarhide

| Date | Activity | Results |
|------|----------|---------|
| 4/3/79 | Several hours were spent looking through the MARYLAND ARCHIVES volumes at Hall of Records, Annapolis, MD. In search of Francis DOLLAHYDE, member of Legislative Assembly, Colonial Maryland, 1701-1722. | Vol. 1  Nothing<br>Vol. 2 & 3  Not Avail.<br>Vol. 4  Nothing<br>Vol. 5,6 & 7  Nothing<br>Vol. 8 & 9  Not Avail.<br>Vol. 10  nothing<br>Vol. 11 & 12  Not avail.<br>Vol. 13  nothing<br>Vol. 14  not avail.<br>Vol. 15 & 16  nothing<br>Vol. 17 & 18  not avail.<br>Vol. 19 thru 25  nothing |
|  | Vol. 26: Francis DOLLAHYDE, in house of Delegates. See pp. 48, 63, 64, 74, 97, 99, 104, 120, 132, 148, 164, 185, 207, 377, 380, 382, 389, 401, 403, 457, 476, 482, 498, 501, 532, 533, 543, 548, 550, 561, 579, 580, 599, 606, 610, 618, and 638 | Vol. 26!  See RFDS ✳<br>shts.<br>[DOLLAHIDE. MD] |
|  | Vol. 27: Francis DOLLAHYDE  p. 61, 66<br>p. 61: "at general Assembly for the Province of Maryland ... 26 Mar. 1707"<br><br>p. 66 Francis, commissioned to serve in the office of <u>High Sheriff</u> of Balto Co MD. | Vol. 28  Nothing<br>Vol. 29  "<br>Vol. 30!  See RFDS ✳<br>shts.<br>Vol. 31, 32  Nothing<br>Vol. 33!  See RFDS ✳<br>Vol. 34!  "  "  ✳<br>Vol. 35  Nothing<br>"<br>" |
|  | Vol. 30: Francis DOLLAHIDE. See pp. 64, 71, 85, 87, 89, 95, 107, 160, 162, 176, 190, 219, 360, 477, 479, 481, 515, 554, 556, 573, 574, 583. | " |
|  | Vol. 33: Fr. DOLLAHIDE. See pp. 54, 70, 201, 220, 227, 255, 271, 365, 386, 505, 507, 565, 592, 594. | Order copies of pages with any genealogical info. of value. (most did nothing except prove he lived there for several years.. |
|  | Vol. 34: "Cap^t Frd. DALLAHIDE" member from Balto Co MD, session begun on 22 Apr 1720 | |
|  | ★ p. 204: "<u>Capt. DOLLAHIDE, deceased.</u>" | ◀ See RFDS MD 47 ★ |
| 4/4/79 | Continuing with <u>Maryland Archives</u>: | Vol. 37 |
|  | Vol. 39: p. 5, 59, & 376: John BRADSHAW petition sent to Lower House. 1732. | |
|  | (John BRADSHAW (Jr.?) Mary, widow of a John Bradshaw, marr. Francis Dollahide (Jr.) ca 1723.) → NO copy made ← | |

# Appendix
# Research Journals and Logs

There are many experts in genealogy who recommend using a "Research Journal" or "Research Calendar" as a diary of work that has been completed. This practice is a good one. However, with the references all collected and filed according to the four basic rules described in Section 2, the positive and potentially positive results have a logical resting place, lessening the need for a journal entry. Nevertheless, a good journal can be very beneficial, if only to avoid repeating unnecessary work. The journal might cross-reference the information stored in the reference collection and, in more detail, describe *negative* results.

In one sense the reference collection filed in surname notebooks should be the main source for results of research. Saving the documents and having them well organized is a constant reminder of what is known and what is not known. But as experienced genealogists have learned, there are always many hours spent in research which produce no positive results. If many hours are spent in fruitless research in a particular book or series of documents, it is worth noting that fact for later.

One method of keeping track of such negative research is to maintain a jour-

nal. The journal need be nothing more than a "diary" type of entry saying that on a certain date work was done on a certain family, but that particular task was a total bust. Letters may have been written, books obtained, or a certain angle of research followed—but the work ended with nothing to add to the project. This is a frustrating experience, and one every genealogist faces constantly. A journal entry can be freestyle, in the style and form most suitable to the genealogist doing the work. A blank sheet of paper will do the job nicely, but certain elements of the journal might be those as shown in the example on page 68. Journal entries can be made in one large collection, serving all surnames being researched—or one journal could be maintained for each surname separately. Again, the genealogist may choose a method that is most suitable to him.

The purpose of the journal is to record the negative results, not the positive results. And if the project for a particular family is reviewed from time to time, it may save repeating work in the future.

Drawbacks to the above journal techniques should be mentioned as well. For example, such a meticulous system may

69

# Correspondence Log

Researcher: _William Dollarhide_

| ITEM NO. | DATE MAILED | MONEY CHK NO. | SUBJECT | REPLY | |
|---|---|---|---|---|---|
| | | | | DATE | RESULTS/ACTION |
| 121 | 2/8/80 | – | Reply to his letter. He sent NEEDHAM/JENNINGS date. Connection not clear – but will keep in touch. | – | no action req'd |
| Sent to Ralph S. HENDERSON 2052 B. Bobcat Langley AFB, VA 23665 | | | | | |
| 122 | 2/9/80 | $4.00 #921 | answered ad in Helper. Sent for "Your Manuscript in Print" | 2/17/80 | rec'd booklet. See File cab. "Printers" |
| Sent to ANUNDSEN PUBLISHING CO. 108 Washington Decorah, iA 52101 | | | | | |
| 123 | 2/9/80 | – | Research in NC Archives. Asked for info, fees, etc.            $ASE | 2/24/80 | Rec'd letter. |
| Sent to Jonathan BUTCHER Box 531 Cary, NC 27511 | | | | | |
| 124 | 2/9/80 | $2.00 #922 | Sent for guide to PA Sources: "The Pennsylvania Line" (1979-80) | 3/1/80 | Rec'd booklet. See "States File"– PA |
| Sent to S.W. PA Gen'l Services PO Box 253-E Laughlintown, PA 15655 | | | | | |
| 125 | 2/12/80 | – | sent for application for membership. Asked for surname check DOLLARHIDE in Randolph CO IN | 2/25/80 | $4.00/year dues. 2 cemetery (index cards) rec'd. SEE RFDS IN43 ! |
| Sent to Randolph Co IN Gen'l Soc. c/o Monisa WISEMAR Route 3- Winchester, IN 47394 | | | | | |
| 126 | 2/13/80 | – | Sent for info & samples of Gen'l computer file, indexing, etc. | 2/28/80 | rec'd material. Do I really want to get into computers ?!? Didn't understand a word of it! |
| Sent to Personalized Computer Svc. 1700 Baywood Dr. #303 Bay City, TX 77414 | | | | | |
| 127 | 3/8/80 | – | Sent info on Philip McNAMER of Ross Co OH 1796-1820. Can he connect? | 4/16/80 | Rec'd letter. Same family! Sent Phillip McNEMAR's will! Gives "son, Noah"!! See (McN.) FANTASTIC NEWS!! RFDS OH21 |
| Sent to Wayne McNAMER Box 565 Lucasville, OH 45648 | | | | | |
| 128 | 5/1/80 | $50.00 #1044 | Sent details re Dollarhides in Randolph Co NC. | 6/11/80 | rec'd report. See RFDS NC 60 thru NC 72. Excellent info! |
| Sent to Jonathan Butcher (See 123) | | | | | |
| 129 | 6/2/80 | – | Sent info re Francis D. in MD. asked for rates. | 6/12 | rec'd letter. will send check. |
| Sent to Anna Cartlidge 362 E. Belvedere Ave. Baltimore, MD 21212 | | | | | |
| 130 | 6/13/80 | $25.00 | Sent check, more data on MD Dollarhides. | 7/2/80 | rec'd letter. Francis D. 1737 in Balto. See RFDS MD 49! |
| Sent to Anna Cartlidge | | | | | |

Sheet No. _12_

not be possible for those "browsers" who love roaming library aisles looking for books of interest. Of course, this practice is limited to those libraries with open shelving where a genealogist can browse through the shelves looking for elusive names and titles that may spark an interest. This type of research, however unprofessional, is enjoyable, but it would be bothersome to write down every book checked, however slight, if the journal system were to be followed faithfully. The type of person who enjoys browsing will probably not be interested in keeping track of every little detail in the research.

## Correspondence Logs

Even if a journal is not maintained, another log—one for keeping track of all letters sent out—can be very worthwhile. A correspondence log need be nothing more than a journal entry, noting the date, the purpose of the letter, and the name and address of the party to whom the letter was mailed. If a check was sent, this is a good place to note that fact as well.

A sample form of a Correspondence Log is shown on page 70. This form was designed to capture the important information for a large letter-writing campaign, keeping the sheets all together in a booklet. In this way it may not be necessary to have an actual copy of every letter written. The value of a correspondence log is having a place where summaries of the letters can be reviewed from time to time to provide a reminder of what was said in the letter or to see which letters need a follow-up.

## Journals and Logs:
### Pass Them on to the Future

The log can also be a place to indicate the success of obtaining certain documents or information through the mail, further indicating where the information is stored in the document files. Well-kept journals and logs give the project life—that is, reading the logs in the future always gives a better insight into how the work reached its present state.

Editorial comments about the quality of the letters received make for excellent reading years after the fact. The log also could become an excellent review of the project by a great-grandchild who reads it decades from now. Logs can become valuable assets to anyone taking over the project in the future. The most successful journals and logs are those written with that potential use in mind.

❀   ❀   ❀   ❀   ❀

# Master Forms

All of the master forms listed below can be used on most photocopying machines with good results. The shaded lines and backgrounds can be lightened by adjusting the dark/light setting on most photocopiers, and the user can experiment with the best settings. Second generation reproductions will tend to cause shaded lines to disappear, leaving straight, handwritten lines in most cases.

List of Forms:

1. Relationship Chart
2. Reference Family Data Sheet (RFDS)
3. Compiled Family Data Sheet (CFDS)
4. Continuation of CFDS
5. Master Data Sheet (MDS)
6. Research Log
7. Ancestor Table
8. Pedigree Ancestor Index
9. Research Journal
10. Correspondence Log

# Important Notice

# Relationship Chart

A relationship between two people can be determined if a common ancestor is known. The two lineages should both begin with the common ancestor, shown on the chart as number 1. Next, list two lineages, one line shown below as A2, A3, A4, etc., which moves up, and the other as B2, B3, B4, etc., which moves down. By tracing any two persons to a point in the box where the grey or white bands intersect, a legal relationship can be found. For example, A3 and B3 are first cousins, but A3 and B4 are first cousins, once removed.

LEGEND:

    N = niece or nephew to uncle or aunt.

    GN = Great niece or nephew.

2C 1R = second cousins, once removed.

3C 4R = third cousins, four times removed.

Lineage A (moving up): A2 son/dau, A3 grandson/dau, A4 great grandson/dau, A5 gr-gr grandson/dau, A6 gr-gr-gr grandson/dau, A7 4gr grandson/dau, A8 5gr grandson/dau, A9 6gr grandson/dau, A10 7gr grandson/dau

Lineage B (moving down): B2 son/dau, B3 grandson/dau, B4 great grandson/dau, B5 gr-gr grandson/dau, B6 gr-gr-gr grandson, B7 4gr grandson/dau, B8 5gr grandson/dau, B9 6gr grandson/dau, B10 7gr grandson/dau

| A10 | A9 | A8 | A7 | A6 | A5 | A4 | A3 | A2 | |
|---|---|---|---|---|---|---|---|---|---|
| 7GN | 6GN | 5GN | 4GN | 3GN | 2GN | GN | N | Siblings | B2 |
| 1C 7R | 1C 6R | 1C 5R | 1C 4R | 1C 3R | 1C 2R | 1C 1R | 1st Cousins | N | B3 |
| 2C 6R | 2C 5R | 2C 4R | 2C 3R | 2C 2R | 2C 1R | 2nd Cousins | 1C 1R | GN | B4 |
| 3C 5R | 3C 4R | 3C 3R | 3C 2R | 3C 1R | 3rd Cousins | 2C 1R | 1C 2R | 2GN | B5 |
| 4C 4R | 4C 3R | 4C 2R | 4C 1R | 4th Cousins | 3C 1R | 2C 2R | 1C 3R | 3GN | B6 |
| 5C 3R | 5C 2R | 5C 1R | 5th Cousins | 4C 1R | 3C 2R | 2C 3R | 1C 4R | 4GN | B7 |
| 6C 2R | 6C 1R | 6th Cousins | 5C 1R | 4C 2R | 3C 3R | 2C 4R | 1C 5R | 5GN | B8 |
| 7C 1R | 7th Cousins | 6C 1R | 5C 2R | 4C 3R | 3C 4R | 2C 5R | 1C 6R | 6GN | B9 |
| 8th Cousins | 7C 1R | 6C 2R | 5C 3R | 4C 4R | 3C 5R | 2C 6R | 1C 7R | 7GN | B10 |

# Reference
## Family Data Sheet

SURNAME | RFDS NUMBER | Sheet......of.......

Date:     Researcher:

**The following data was taken from a single source exactly as it was found.**

**Source of data**

☐ Book    ☐ Periodical    ☐ Film    ☐ Other*    | Author/Editor:

Title/Article:

In/By:      Vol.    No.    Page    Pub.

Data was obtained from the following:   ☐ Library research   ☐ Correspondence**   ☐ Field research   ☐ Oral dictation   ☐ Fam. rec'ds   ☐ Other*

**Census only**

☐ Soundex    ☐ Schedules    ☐ Mortality   |   ☐ Printed   ☐ Microfilm  |  Roll No.     Page     Fam. No.

Year     State     County        Township        Subdistrict

*Other Information:          ☐ Indexe

**From

# Compiled
## Family Data Sheet

Compiled By: _____  Updated: _____

This sheet is a composite of _____ REFERENCE Family Data Sheets, which are itemized on the reverse side of this sheet.

## HUSBAND

| ID No. | Full Name | DATE OF BIRTH | day | month | year |
|---|---|---|---|---|---|

Other Names or Nicknames

Physical Description

child of _____ children. No. of brothers _____ No. of sisters _____

Other details

| PLACE OF BIRTH | Town |
| | Township |
| | County |
| | State/Country |

**HIS DEATH**

Date of death _____ Cause _____ Died at the age of _____ years, _____ months, _____ days

Place of death

Mortuary / Cemetery

| HIS FATHER | born | died | CFDS NO. |
| HIS MOTHER | born | died | |

**MARRIAGE DATA**

Marriage recorded in Book _____ Page _____ of the County of _____ State of _____

☐ Church record   ☐ Bible record   DATE OF MARRIAGE: _____

Place of ceremony

Performed by

His other marriage(s)

Her other marriage(s)

## WIFE

| ID No. | Full Maiden Name | DATE OF BIRTH | day | month | year |
|---|---|---|---|---|---|

Other Names or Nicknames

Physical Description

child of _____ children. No. of brothers _____ No. of sisters _____

Other details

| PLACE OF BIRTH | Town |
| | Township |
| | County |
| | State/Country |

**HER DEATH**

Date of death _____ Cause _____ Died at the age of _____ years, _____ months, _____ days

Place of death

Mortuary / Cemetery

| HER FATHER | born | died | CFDS NO. |
| HER MOTHER | born | died | |

## Children (Given Names)

| Children (Given Names) | b: Birth Date / m: Marriage Date / d: Death Date | PLACE OF EVENT | SPOUSE | CFDS NO. |
|---|---|---|---|---|
| 1 | b | | | |
| | m | | | |
| | d | | | |
| 2 | b | | | |
| | m | | | |
| | d | | | |
| 3 | b | | | |
| | m | | | |
| | d | | | |
| 4 | b | | | |
| | m | | | |
| | d | | | |
| 5 | b | | | |
| | m | | | |
| | d | | | |
| 6 | b | | | |
| | m | | | |
| | d | | | |
| 7 | b | | | |
| | m | | | |
| | d | | | |
| 8 | b | | | |
| | m | | | |
| | d | | | |

| Children (Given Names) | b : m : d : Birth Date Marriage Date Death Date | | PLACE OF EVENT | SPOUSE | CFDS NO. |
|---|---|---|---|---|---|
| 9 | b | | | | |
| | m | | | | |
| | d | | | | |
| 10 | b | | | | |
| | m | | | | |
| | d | | | | |
| 11 | b | | | | |
| | m | | | | |
| | d | | | | |
| 12 | b | | | | |
| | m | | | | |
| | d | | | | |
| 13 | b | | | | |
| | m | | | | |
| | d | | | | |
| 14 | b | | | | |
| | m | | | | |
| | d | | | | |

The following is a list of all source material concerning this family which has been found to date. For full details, refer to the REFERENCE Family Data Sheets (RFDS) itemized below. Each RFDS is filed by surname, place and sheet number.

| Item No. | Reference Family Data Sheet | | Type of Record | In Reference to | Information Given |
|---|---|---|---|---|---|
| | Surname | State/No. | | | |
| | | | | | |
| | | | | | |
| | | | | | |
| | | | | | |
| | | | | | |
| | | | | | |
| | | | | | |
| | | | | | |
| | | | | | |
| | | | | | |
| | | | | | |
| | | | | | |
| | | | | | |
| | | | | | |
| | | | | | |
| | | | | | |
| | | | | | |

# Master Data Sheet
## For One Pedigree Ancestor

| NAME | | ANCESTOR NUMBER | |
|---|---|---|---|

Researcher:

The following information concerns one person – a pedigree ancestor. Refer to Research Log for this person for an itemized list of sources. See Family Group sheet for details concerning this person's spouse, children, and all family births, deaths and marriages.

| FULL NAME AT TIME OF BIRTH | | BIRTH DATE | day ____ month ____ year |
|---|---|---|---|
| Other names, including nicknames: | | PLACE OF BIRTH | Town/City |
| Physical description: | | | Township |
| Child of ____ children. Number of brothers: ____ Number of sisters: ____ | | | County |
| Church records: | | | State/Country |

| MARRIAGE DATA | Name of spouse: | Ancestor No. |
|---|---|---|
| | Married at: | |
| | ____ of ____ marriages. Date of license: ____ Date of ceremony: ____ | |
| | Marriage performed by: ____ Title: ____ | |
| | Witnesses: | |
| | Names of children of above marriage: | |
| | | |
| | Other marriages: | |

| DEATH | Date of death ____ cause ____ at age of ____ years, ____ months, ____ days |
|---|---|
| | Place of death / burial: |
| | Undertaker / cemetery: |

| PROBATE | Jurisdiction: |
|---|---|
| | Disposition: |

**REMARKS**

# Research Log
## For One Pedigree Ancestor

| NAME | | ANCESTOR NUMBER | |
|------|--|-----------------|--|

Researcher:

The following data represents every research item that has been found about one person.

| LOG NO. | Reference Family Data Sheet | | Type of Record | Information Given |
|---------|------------------|----------|----------------|-------------------|
| | Surname | State/No | | |
| | | | | |
| | | | | |
| | | | | |
| | | | | |
| | | | | |
| | | | | |
| | | | | |
| | | | | |
| | | | | |
| | | | | |
| | | | | |
| | | | | |
| | | | | |
| | | | | |
| | | | | |
| | | | | |
| | | | | |
| | | | | |
| | | | | |
| | | | | |
| | | | | |
| | | | | |
| | | | | |
| | | | | |
| | | | | |

# Ancestor Table

**First Pedigree Ancestor with this Surname.**

Married→

**Father**

Born _____ Where _____ When _____
Died _____ Where _____ Where _____

Married→

**Grandfather**

Born _____ Where _____ When _____
Died _____ Where _____ Where _____

Married→

Born _____ Where _____ When _____
Died _____ Where _____ Where _____

Married→

Born _____ Where _____ When _____
Died _____ Where _____ Where _____

Married→

Born _____ Where _____ When _____
Died _____ Where _____ Where _____

Married→

Born _____ Where _____ When _____
Died _____ Where _____ Where _____

Married→

Born _____ Where _____ When _____
Died _____ Where _____ Where _____

Married→

Born _____ Where _____ When _____
Died _____ Where _____ Where _____

Married→

Born _____ Where _____ When _____
Died _____ Where _____ Where _____

Married→

Born _____ Where _____ When _____
Died _____ Where _____ Where _____

Married→

Born _____ Where _____ When _____
Died _____ Where _____ Where _____

Married→

Born _____ Where _____ When _____
Died _____ Where _____ Where _____

Married→

Born _____ Where _____ When _____
Died _____ Where _____ Where _____

# Pedigree Ancestor Index

Father

Mother

Each known ancestor in this generation
is repeated and starts a new sheet.

The first person
on this sheet is
ANCESTOR NO.

# Research Journal

| Date | Activity | Results |
|------|----------|---------|
|      |          |         |

# Correspondence Log

Researcher:

| ITEM NO. | DATE MAILED | MONEY CHK NO. | SUBJECT | REPLY | |
|---|---|---|---|---|---|
| | | | | DATE | RESULTS/ACTION |
| Sent to | | | | | |
| Sent to | | | | | |
| Sent to | | | | | |
| Sent to | | | | | |
| Sent to | | | | | |
| Sent to | | | | | |
| Sent to | | | | | |
| Sent to | | | | | |
| Sent to | | | | | |
| Sent to | | | | | |

Sheet No.